22.71

RC
i 1
'93
~09

D0456929

Anxiety Disorders

Titles in the Diseases and Disorders series include:

Acne
AIDS
Allergies
Alzheimer's Disease
Anorexia and Bulimia
Anthrax
Arthritis
Asthma
Attention Deficit Disorder
Autism
Bipolar Disorder
Birth Defects
Blindness
Brain Tumors
Breast Cancer
Cerebral Palsy
Chronic Fatigue Syndrome
Cystic Fibrosis
Deafness
Diabetes
Down Syndrome
Dyslexia
The Ebola Virus
Epilepsy
Fetal Alcohol Syndrome
Flu
Food Poisoning
Growth Disorders
Headaches
Heart Disease

Hemophilia
Hepatitis
Hodgkin's Disease
Human Papillomavirus (HPV)
Leukemia
Lou Gehrig's Disease
Lyme Disease
Mad Cow Disease
Malaria
Malnutrition
Measles and Rubella
Meningitis
Mental Retardation
Multiple Sclerosis
Muscular Dystrophy
Obesity
Ovarian Cancer
Parkinson's Disease
Phobias
Prostate Cancer
SARS
Schizophrenia
Sexually Transmitted
   Diseases
Sleep Disorders
Smallpox
Strokes
Teen Depression
Tuberculosis
West Nile Virus

DISEASES & DISORDERS

Anxiety Disorders

Sheila Wyborny

LUCENT BOOKS

A part of Gale, Cengage Learning

GALE
CENGAGE Learning™

New York • San Francisco • New Haven, Conn • Waterville, Maine • London

GALE
CENGAGE Learning

LIBRARY OF CONGRESS CATALOGING-IN-PUBLICATION DATA

Wyborny, Sheila, 1950
  Anxiety disorders / By Sheila Wyborny.
    p. cm. — (Diseases and disorders)
  Includes bibliographical references and index.
  ISBN 978-1-4205-0071-4 (hardcover)
  1. Anxiety—Juvenile literature. 2. Phobias—Juvenile literature.
3. Panic disorders—Juvenile literature. 4. Post–traumatic stress
disorder—Juvenile literature. I. Title.
  RC531.W93 2009
  616.85'22—dc22
                                                    2008025704

Lucent Books
27500 Drake Rd.
Farmington Hills, MI 48331

ISBN-13: 978-1-4205-0071-4
ISBN-10: 1-4205-0071-6

Printed in the United States of America
1 2 3 4 5 6 7 12 11 10 09 08

Table of Contents

"The Most Difficult Puzzles Ever Devised"

Charles Best, one of the pioneers in the search for a cure for diabetes, once explained what it is about medical research that intrigued him so. "It's not just the gratification of knowing one is helping people," he confided, "although that probably is a more heroic and selfless motivation. Those feelings may enter in, but truly, what I find best is the feeling of going toe to toe with nature, of trying to solve the most difficult puzzles ever devised. The answers are there somewhere, those keys that will solve the puzzle and make the patient well. But how will those keys be found?"

Since the dawn of civilization, nothing has so puzzled people—and often frightened them, as well—as the onset of illness in a body or mind that had seemed healthy before. A seizure, the inability of a heart to pump, the sudden deterioration of muscle tone in a small child—being unable to reverse such conditions or even to understand why they occur was unspeakably frustrating to healers. Even before there were names for such conditions, even before they were understood at all, each was a reminder of how complex the human body was, and how vulnerable.

While our grappling with understanding diseases has been frustrating at times, it has also provided some of humankind's most heroic accomplishments. Alexander Fleming's accidental discovery in 1928 of a mold that could be turned into penicillin has resulted in the saving of untold millions of lives. The isolation of the enzyme insulin has reversed what was once a death sentence for anyone with diabetes. There have been great strides in combating conditions for which there is not yet a cure, too. Medicines can help AIDS patients live longer, diagnostic tools such as mammography and ultrasounds can help doctors find tumors while they are treatable, and laser surgery techniques have made the most intricate, minute operations routine.

This "toe-to-toe" competition with diseases and disorders is even more remarkable when seen in a historical continuum. An astonishing amount of progress has been made in a very short time. Just two hundred years ago, the existence of germs as a cause of some diseases was unknown. In fact, it was less than 150 years ago that a British surgeon named Joseph Lister had difficulty persuading his fellow doctors that washing their hands before delivering a baby might increase the chances of a healthy delivery (especially if they had just attended to a diseased patient)!

Each book in Lucent's Diseases and Disorders series explores a disease or disorder and the knowledge that has been accumulated (or discarded) by doctors through the years. Each book also examines the tools used for pinpointing a diagnosis, as well as the various means that are used to treat or cure a disease. Finally, new ideas are presented—techniques or medicines that may be on the horizon.

Frustration and disappointment are still part of medicine, for not every disease or condition can be cured or prevented. But the limitations of knowledge are being pushed outward constantly; the "most difficult puzzles ever devised" are finding challengers every day.

When Anxiety Becomes a Disorder

T he boy approached the crumbling old house. The place looked depressing in the daylight, but now, at night, it was downright creepy. He looked back over his shoulder at his friends, hiding behind the tall stone fence. They peeked around the gatepost as he reluctantly approached the house, stumbling on the broken flagstones of the walkway. Stupid, stupid, stupid! He should not have taken their dare. The closer he got to the house, the more frightening it looked. Although it was a chilly night, he could feel perspiration dripping down his back. He forced himself to climb the rickety steps to the porch. His hands shook as he pushed open the warped door, which creaked eerily on its rusty hinges. Hesitantly, he stepped across the threshold. He tried to swallow, but his mouth was too dry. Then he heard it! A low moaning, groaning sound. His mind told his legs to get him out of that place, but at first his feet refused to move. Finally, though, his body obeyed his brain and he dashed out the door. It was only 50 feet (17m) to the front gate, but by the time he collapsed against the stone column, his heart was pounding and his breath was coming in short gasps as though he had run a marathon.

In a relatively short span of time, the boy had experienced several symptoms of anxiety. Basically, it was all about fear and not wanting his friends to know he was afraid. Finally, though, the moaning and groaning pushed his fear to the point that he was more afraid of whatever was making the sound than he was of what his friends would think.

Ordinary Emotions

Fear and anxiety are common emotions in adults, teens, and children. Many children fear faceless monsters in the dark corners of their closets and under their beds. In fact, several

Fear and anxiety are common emotions in people of all ages and are often experienced by young children on the first day of kindergarten or day care.

children's books have been written about these imaginary crea-
tures. Babies and young children often cling to their parents
and cry hysterically the first day of day care or kindergarten,
fearing that their parents will not come back to get them or
that something might happen to their parents after they leave.
Parents face separation anxiety issues of their own at these
times. They may feel guilty for leaving their children and may
fear that something bad might happen to their children while
they are away.

Older children and teens may feel anxious when they sit
down to take a test or have sweaty palms and rapid heartbeats
when they try out for a school play, the cheerleading squad, the
debate team, or a sports team. Adults experience similar symptoms when they face job interviews or when their employers
call them in for a performance review. Other situations, like
having a tax audit or being stopped for a speeding ticket, can
also cause stress and anxiety.

Basically, a certain amount of stress and anxiety are normal parts of life. As long as there have been people on Earth,
there has been anxiety. The primitive "fight or flight" emotions
were experienced by ancient people when they faced danger,
whether it was an enemy wielding a heavy club or a loud clap
of thunder. People respond to threats against their safety, welfare, or happiness with anxiety. When animals face threats to
their safety, they experience anxiety and stress, as well. Anxiety is a normal emotion.

Normal in Kids; Unusual in Adults

Some people respond to normal events and situations with
excessive anxiety, though, and may exhibit behaviors that
seem unusual. For instance, while it is natural for children
to play the "step on a crack and break your mother's back"
game as they walk down a sidewalk, if an adult obsessively
avoids stepping on cracks, this behavior could be related to
an anxiety disorder. Another relatively common childhood behavior is to carefully separate foods on the plate and not allow
different foods to come into contact with each other. A second

food-related issue concerns portions. Sometimes at the family table, children compare their portions with those of their brothers or sisters to be sure their parents are not showing favoritism by short-changing their portions. Parents may find this behavior annoying, but they tend to accept it as a childish quirk.

For adults who continue with the same sort of behavior, not allowing foods to touch or obsessively checking and rechecking portion sizes, this can be a symptom of an anxiety disorder. Some people divide their foods according to color, size of portions, or texture. They may further divide each portion into a mathematically calculated number of bites, insist on separate forks for each food, and have a certain number of napkins with their table setting. They may use the napkins to wipe each knife, fork, and spoon a certain number of times. They may even chew each bite according to some mathematical formula. Such behavior crosses the line from being mildly peculiar to obsessive.

In Distinguished Company

People of any race, ethnic group, religion, or income level can be affected by anxiety disorders. In some instances, famous people from earlier times have been diagnosed with anxiety disorders many years after their deaths. One of these is poet Alfred, Lord Tennyson (1809–1892). He once described his feelings of extreme panic and anxiety and his hopes for improvement shortly before he began a controversial treatment program of wet sheets and cold baths: "The perpetual panic and horror of the last two years had steeped my nerves in poison; now I am left a beggar but am or shall be shortly somewhat better off in nerves."[1] Despite this treatment and others, though, he continued to experience what was then called nervous illness throughout his life.

In addition to Tennyson, another literary giant of the time, Charlotte Brontë, suffered from similar nervous disorders. Brontë, the author of *Jane Eyre*, was troubled by periods of anxiety and depression. Treatments to remedy her condition were also unsuccessful. For instance, she was treated with oral

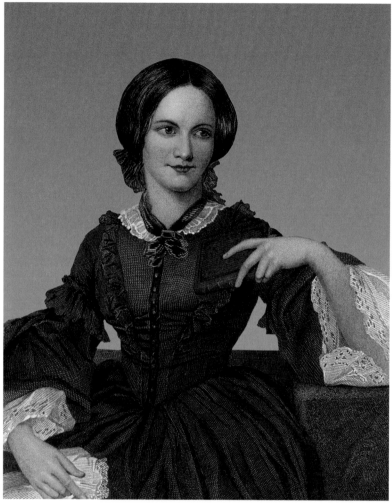

English novelist Charlotte Brontë suffered from bouts of anxiety and depression throughout her life and tried several treatments with no success.

doses of the heavy metal, mercury, which made her become violently ill.

Scientist and inventor, Nikola Tesla (1856–1943), inventor of radio, fluorescent lighting, and missile science, suffered from several different nervous disorders. It is believed his were triggered by the death of his older brother, when Tesla was five years old. He developed phobias and a number of compulsions and was also troubled by symptoms similar to panic attacks. Tesla spoke of his maladies: "This caused me great discomfort and anxiety. . . . None of the students of psychology of physiology whom I have consulted could ever explain satisfactorily these phenomena."[2]

Out in the Open

A number of present-day celebrities openly discuss their experiences with anxiety disorders. Among these famous people are actress Drew Barrymore and celebrity chef and entrepreneur Paula Deen. In 2006 Barrymore publicly discussed being troubled by panic attacks. Deen described her experiences with agoraphobia, fear of leaving home, in her 2007 autobiography, *It Ain't All About the Cookin'*.

By going public with their experiences, these widely recognized celebrities have demonstrated to average people suffering from anxiety disorders that these conditions are not shameful secrets to be hidden. Instead, they are genuine medical illnesses that can be diagnosed and treated, and that with proper treatment, people affected by these conditions can have normal, emotionally healthy lives.

CHAPTER ONE

What Are Anxiety Disorders?

The word *anxiety* comes from a Greek term meaning "to press tight" or "to strangle." In Latin, the word *anxius* means constriction, or discomfort. In any language, periods of anxiety, even under normal conditions, can trigger a combination of unpleasant symptoms. These symptoms may include shaking hands, upset stomach, tightness in the neck and shoulders, tightness in the chest, heavy perspiration, rapid heartbeat, and dry mouth. Everyone, young and old, has experienced some of these symptoms of anxiety at some time. Anxiety can be a healthy emotion. It can serve as a warning that a situation may not be safe, and it would be better to leave a certain place than hang around and risk the consequences. Anxiety, under these conditions, is reasonable and normal.

However, when anxiety crosses the line from reasonable and normal to excessive and obsessive it becomes a mental disorder, or an anxiety disorder. By definition, anxiety disorders are a group of abnormal fears and nervous conditions, also called anxiety neuroses, which are triggered when a person finds himself or herself in fearful situations. These emotions and behaviors could be caused by a fear of heights, crowds, taking tests, spiders, or even something as nonthreatening as a piece of chalk, a balloon, or a paper clip.

Anxiety disorders are the most common form of mental illness. According to some estimates, some forms of anxiety

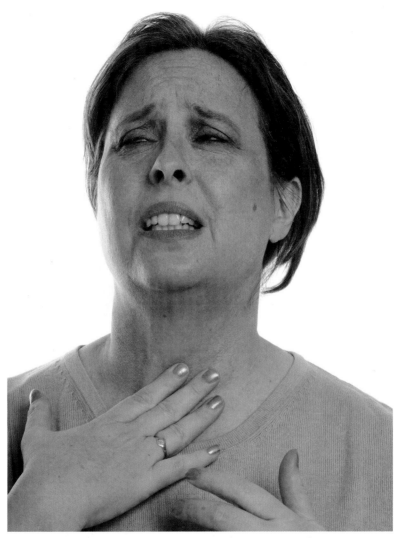

A woman experiencing an anxiety attack, sometimes known as a panic attack. Anxiety disorders can be triggered by biological factors or stressful events.

disorders may affect as many as 40 million Americans over the age of eighteen each year. Up to 17 percent of the adult population suffers from some type of anxiety disorder. In fact, many people experience different degrees of anxiety disorders and are not even aware of it. For instance, if a person crosses the street to avoid seeing a snake in a pet shop window, that person may have a type of anxiety disorder called a phobia. If another person collects something, like spoons, and there are hundreds of spoons on every surface in every room of the person's home, this person may have an obsession. These, though, are fairly mild examples. Anxiety disorders may result from a variety of causes. Biologically, anxiety disorders can be caused by abnormalities in brain chemistry or may be inherited. On the other hand, they can also be triggered by stressful events in a person's life or by prolonged periods of stress. Whatever the cause, though, anxiety disorders in their extreme states can seriously interfere with a person's life. They can get in the way of family relationships and affect careers.

Anxiety disorders fall into five basic categories. These disorders have been classified according to specific behavioral characteristics. These categories are generalized anxiety disorder, phobias, obsessive-compulsive disorder, panic attacks and panic disorder, and post-traumatic stress disorder. These disorders can range from mild to extreme, and a person can be affected by one type of anxiety disorder or more than one of these disorders at the same time.

Generalized Anxiety Disorder

Generalized anxiety disorder (GAD) sufferers account for about 3 percent of all anxiety disorders. GAD is characterized by constant worries and fears, which in some cases get in the way of a person's ability to function normally on a daily basis. GAD sufferers are almost always anxious about something, and they might not even know why. They may feel generally restless and anxious about nearly anything and either have difficulty controlling their worries or cannot control or break free of them at all. They worry excessively about things, such as their job, health, family, relationships, and the weather, and catastrophize, or dwell, on worst-case scenarios. For instance, if a person with GAD is hired for a new job, he might worry excessively that he is doomed to failure. In fact, he might do

Some common symptoms of generalized anxiety disorder, or GAD, are difficulty sleeping and headaches.

such a good job of convincing himself that he is going to fail, that he could ultimately lose the job.

People with GAD tend to feel "keyed up" most of the time and have difficulty concentrating on any subject. Sometimes, their minds simply go blank. They are often tired, have trouble sleeping, suffer from headaches, and experience muscle tension, or what they may describe as knots in their muscles. GAD can produce symptoms such as sweating, nausea, dizziness, and the need to make frequent trips to the bathroom.

Many people suffering from GAD use defense mechanisms to cope with their problems. Some may try to hide or disguise the condition. Some blame others for their anxieties. A young person with GAD may say teachers and other students are picking on him and causing his worries or blame a sibling for his feelings. An adult might say his boss has it in for him. They may express their frustration in anger. In extreme cases, the anger could turn to violence.

Denial is another defense mechanism. The person may tell others that he has no problem with anxiety. He might even deny it to himself. People who use these defense mechanisms are not actually dealing their problems, though. They are merely putting off facing their condition and getting help for it.

One person described a period of time when GAD was at its worst: "I'd have terrible sleeping problems. There were times I'd wake up wired in the middle of the night. I had trouble concentrating, even reading the newspaper or a novel. Sometimes I'd feel a little light headed. My heart would race or pound. And that would make me worry more. I was always imagining things were worse than they really were; when I got a stomachache, I'd think it was cancer."[3]

Experts disagree on some points about GAD. Some medical professionals believe that GAD is more of a trait than an actual condition and that GAD can get worse and develop into a specific type of anxiety disorder, such as a phobia. However, other medical experts believe that GAD is an independent disorder and should be treated on the basis of its own symptoms.

Regardless of how it is classified, GAD affects the lives of more than a million Americans each year. Frequently, it comes on slowly over a period of time. It can come on so slowly that sometimes the person is not aware of the condition until it is seriously affecting the person's daily life. A diagnosis of GAD is usually made after the person seeking help has been in a state of excessive worry for about six months. In a mild state, people with GAD can function normally on the job and in social situations, but in extreme cases, the patient may be in a serious emotional state and have difficulty getting along in any situation. However, unlike some anxiety disorders, people with GAD usually do not avoid situations that could trigger an emotional response. Additionally, GAD is sometimes accompanied by other serious problems, such as depression or substance abuse.

Phobias

Of all the anxiety disorders, many experts believe that phobias are the most common, thereby making phobia the most common type of mental disorder in the United States. Many people fear certain objects or situations, but when these fears become so extreme that they interfere with daily activities,

The fear of spiders is a common specific phobia experienced by people and is more than a dislike of spiders. A spider phobia is an intense, irrational, unexplainable fear of spiders, even when one might not be present.

they have become a phobia. A medical diagnosis of phobia is usually made when the person has experienced symptoms for six months or more. Phobias involve intense, irrational, or unexplainable fears. These fears can be associated with objects, animals, insects, people, situations, or places. Most phobias are associated with things that pose little or no danger. The person does not even have to be in the presence of the source of the phobia to trigger it. Seeing the object of the fear in a picture or on television or even the thought of coming in contact with it is often enough to cause a reaction.

Since phobias take so many forms, they have been classified into three basic types: specific phobias, social phobias, and agoraphobia. Some people are affected by two or more types of phobias at the same time. For instance, a person might have a social phobia, such as a fear of dining in restaurants, and a specific phobia, like a fear of spiders.

People with social phobias are afraid of being embarrassed, criticized, or attracting some other type of negative attention in public places or situations. Social phobias include the fear of speaking in public and any activity that would place a person at the center of attention. People with this type of phobia tend to be shy and introverted. They often do not look people in the eye when they speak with them. They avoid parties and other group events. Because of this condition, they will avoid crowded places like shopping malls and theaters. Their fears may prevent them from using public transportation, like buses or subways, and will even cause them to put off going to the bank or the grocery store until they are completely out of money or food.

Specific phobias can be broken down into several categories. Animal phobia is the fear of animals or insects. Natural environment phobias involve a fear of storms, heights, darkness, or water. People who have an abnormal fear of having blood tests or getting injections suffer from blood-injection type phobia. Situational type phobias can be triggered by different types of transportation, like automobiles, airplanes, or buses, or enclosed places like tunnels or elevators. There is even a category for phobias that do not fit in any of the other categories. This category is called "other type." It includes fear of illness or disease, doctors, dentists, and loud noises, and costume characters, like clowns, among others.

A fear of heights, flying, being in a small space, snakes, and insects are fairly common specific phobias, but people can also have phobic reactions to something as nonthreatening as balloons, a type of vegetable, pencils, chalk, or even certain numbers. Both children and adults with unusual specific phobias are often teased and laughed at, but phobias are no laughing matter. Like any mental disorder, they can seriously disrupt a person's life, put jobs at risk, and damage or destroy relationships. Left untreated, they can lead to serious depression, drug or alcohol addiction, or even suicide.

Lucky Thirteen?

Sarah Pardee Winchester, heir to the Winchester rifle fortune, had some serious obsessions. Following the death of her husband and child, she moved to San Jose, California, where she purchased a large eight-room house. She began renovating the house immediately. In fact, renovations continued 24 hours a day, 7 days a week, 365 days a year, for the remaining 38 years of her life. By the time of her death, on September 5, 1922, the 8-room house had grown to 160 rooms. Some believe Mrs. Winchester was obsessed with ghosts, and it was the ghosts, communicating through séances, who compelled her to keep building.

Another of Mrs. Winchester's obsessions was the number thirteen. Staircases in her remarkable house have thirteen steps, rooms have thirteen windows, and windows have thirteen panes. There are thirteen chandeliers with thirteen lights, and there are also thirteen bathrooms in the house. When Mrs. Winchester's will was read following her death, it was discovered that it was written in thirteen sections and signed thirteen times.

The third general type of phobia is agoraphobia. Agoraphobia is a complex anxiety disorder. It is characterized by extreme fear and anxiety associated with being in a place or a situation in which people fear they will lose their self-control, that they may, for instance, suddenly behave in a bizarre manner. They are afraid they will have no help if they should become dizzy, faint, or experience any other potentially embarrassing anxiety symptoms. On the surface, agoraphobia may appear similar to social phobia, but there are differences. People with social phobias become anxious in social situations or fear committing some sort of social error in public. Basically, they fear the reactions of others. Agoraphobics, however, have a morbid fear of totally losing control of their actions and not having someone to help them if they do.

Obsessive-Compulsive Disorder

Obsessive-compulsive disorder (OCD) is similar to other anxiety disorders in that the person may be obsessed with troublesome thoughts or worries that prey on the mind and sometimes prevent the person from functioning normally. For instance, someone may have a persistent fear that a door has been left unlocked so burglars might get in or that the stove or the coffeemaker has been left on, which might start a fire and burn down the house. Some OCD sufferers have a morbid fear of harming someone or of catching a serious disease.

The other half of this disorder is compulsion. The person's fears compel him or her to perform certain rituals or a repetitive behavior. Repeated hand washing, leaving and entering a room a certain number of times, or turning lights on and off a certain number of times are examples of compulsive behavior. The person fears that something bad will happen if these rituals are not performed or he or she may perform the rituals to make a bad feeling go away. The compulsive behavior may relieve the bad feeling, but only temporarily. When the tension returns, the person will feel compelled to perform the ritualistic behavior again. It becomes a self-destructive cycle.

As part of obsessive-compulsive disorder, a person might feel the need to perform rituals, like turning the light on and off a certain number of times before entering a room.

One OCD sufferer, a man, described how intense some of his compulsions became: "I switched the light switch on and off at least a hundred times. I would check under my bed every night. I checked the zipper on my pants to see if it was open. I always checked the back of my jacket to see if anyone had put a sticker on it. I was very paranoid and felt insecure. I also washed my hands more than needed."[4]

Repetitive actions are not the only behaviors associated with OCD. Some people feel compelled to hoard or collect things. Some of these items may be totally useless, like broken dishes or appliances that cannot be repaired. Hanging onto materials, like old magazines, newspapers, or junk mail until it fills large spaces in the home and becomes a health or fire hazard, is a potentially dangerous compulsion. Some OCD sufferers simply cannot get rid of anything. They are unable to donate or give away still-useful items they no longer need. Hoarders sometimes collect objects until there is literally no room left to live normally. Hoarders who live in apartments may be evicted, because their hoarding has become a safety or a health hazard. Purchasing items far beyond what is needed or can be used is also a form of hoarding. For instance, instead of purchasing a six-roll package of paper towels and then going back to the store and buying more when he runs out, the hoarder might buy two or three cases of paper towels, bathroom tissue, or cleaning products and stack them in the corner of the dining room or the garage.

Some compulsive behaviors involve trying to be perfect, trying to do things perfectly, or trying to create a perfect environment. These compulsive behaviors include excessive cleaning or ordering and arranging items in the environment. People who are obsessed with being perfect or doing things perfectly might keep new purchases unused and in their original packages for months or years. These people may avoid using closets or rooms once they have been perfectly arranged. They may need to arrange items in storage in a certain order, like arranging the cans on the pantry shelf in pairs or symmetrical arrangements, and become upset if someone comes along and moves the items.

Another way people can become obsessed with perfection is with their own bodies. This form of OCD is called body dismorphic disorder, or BDD. This disorder might be something fairly mild, such as frequently checking one's appearance in the mirror, but it can also escalate until it takes a toll on the person's health, both mentally and physically. These people may become obsessed about being overweight or underweight or dwell on parts of their bodies they feel are less than perfect.

Cheyenne Cawthon of Illinois has body dysmorphic disorder, or BDD. Because of this disorder, she finds that she has a distorted image of her body when in reality her body is fine.

Some seek to remedy these imperfections, real or imagined, with plastic surgery, or reconstructive surgery. Once people with BDD start having these operations, they sometimes cannot stop. They become addicted to changing their bodies surgically until they look less like human beings and more like mannequins in the windows of department stores.

Some people with BDD become obsessed with their own bodies in other ways, as well. Some obsessions, like picking, can become destructive. For instance, some people with this condition literally mutilate their bodies in a variety of ways. These people may pull out their own hair from their heads, eyebrows, or eyelashes. They may pick at their skin or even bite themselves until they bleed. They may also bite their nails into the quick, chew their cuticles, or pick at pimples until they bleed or become infected.

At one time, OCD was thought to be a relatively rare disorder. In the 1950s, only about 0.05 percent of adult Americans were diagnosed with it. Since then, though, the numbers have grown. In fact, by 1985, that figure had grown to 2.5 percent, and, according to studies done by Columbia University Medical Center and Villanova University, OCD sufferers make up about 3 percent of the adult population in the United States. This is about 5 million people.

Animals and OCD

Obsessive-compulsive disorder (OCD) affects dogs, as well as humans. In fact, certain breeds of dogs are more likely to be affected by OCD than others. For example, German shepherds tend to chase their own tails, and English bull terriers have the peculiar habit of sticking their heads under things and then standing stock-still, as though hiding. In other breeds, OCD may show up as odd behavior directed at inanimate objects, such as shoes, food dishes, or bicycles. In cats, OCD is often a peculiar eating behavior. A cat may suck on objects or chew fabric. According to one study, OCD is especially predominate in the Burmese and Siamese breeds.

In both dogs and cats, OCD appears in animals experiencing stressful events and situations. This could be first separations as puppies or kittens. In older animals, OCD could be brought on by a move to a new owner or with a familiar owner to a new home. In dogs, OCD can make a dangerous animal out of a formerly lovable pet. If OCD-like symptoms appear, the cat or dog should be evaluated by a qualified veterinarian before any serious damage to the pet, owners, or property can occur.

People who experience panic attacks on the way to school or work may avoid going to these places in the future.

Panic Attacks and Panic Disorder

Panic is an overpowering feeling of fear. People who have panic attacks are overcome with fear and experience physical symptoms such as shortness of breath, rapid heartbeat, nausea, trembling, choking, numbness in the hands, and nausea. Possibly the worst thing about panic attacks and panic disorders is that people have no control over when they will occur. They can come on suddenly with little or no warning and are terrifying. During these attacks, people will usually experience fifteen to thirty minutes of these symptoms. Like people with social phobia or agoraphobia, people whose panic attacks occur very frequently and severely may become afraid to leave their homes for fear of one of these attacks coming on in a public place. These people can become self-imposed prisoners vin their own homes.

For some people, the symptoms resemble those of a heart attack. As described by an anonymous source: "It started 10 years ago, when I had just graduated from college and started a new job. I was sitting in a business seminar in a hotel and this thing came out of the blue. I felt like I was dying."[5]

Panic disorder affects nearly 2.5 million adult Americans. However, not everyone who has panic attacks will develop panic disorder. Many people will have just one panic attack and then never experience another. In fact, about one-in-three adult Americans will experience one panic attack at some time in their lives. Panic attacks become disorders when the symptoms, or obsessive worry about those symptoms, persist for a month or more.

However, people who experience panic attacks are less likely to seek help than people with any other emotional disorder. In fact, only 21 percent of the people who suffer from frequent panic attacks seek medical help. Untreated, panic disorder can become a severe disability. Since some of the symptoms are the same as those of a heart attack, people may make several trips to the emergency room or see a number of doctors before the condition is correctly diagnosed.

Like other anxiety disorders, panic disorder can lead to additional serious conditions, such as depression and substance abuse. Sometimes the depression becomes so severe that these people consider suicide. About 90 percent of panic disorder patients have at least one other psychiatric condition, especially phobia. Like certain types of phobias, panic attacks may cause people to avoid the specific places where these attacks tend to occur, which can be especially difficult if these places are along the route to school, work, or other places involved in a person's normal daily routine. For instance, if a person has experienced several attacks in the lobby of the office building where he or she works, it would be difficult if not impossible to get to and from the office. Additionally, if attacks have occurred in a certain classroom, a college student may try to get a schedule change or drop the class.

One person who has experienced these attacks describes this fear: "In between attacks there is this dread and anxiety that it's going to happen again. I'm afraid to go back to places where I've had an attack. Unless I get help, there soon won't be any place where I can go and feel safe from panic."[6]

Post-Traumatic Stress Disorder

The final general category of anxiety disorder is post-traumatic stress disorder (PTSD). PTSD usually results from a life-threatening or some other extremely frightening trauma, such as physical assault. PTSD can also be brought on by a natural disaster, like a hurricane, a tornado, a fire, or a flood. Sometimes, people in the military, especially those returning from combat duty, are diagnosed with this condition.

Like people who suffer from OCD, people suffering from PTSD tend to avoid things that remind them of the experiences that caused the condition. Often, they do not wish to talk about or even think about these events. People with PTSD may become reclusive, avoiding family, friends, and activities, such as sporting events, that they once enjoyed. Like other anxiety disorders, PTSD can plunge people into deep depression or lead to substance abuse, which could require emergency intervention and treatment.

Jesus Bocanegra (center) has been diagnosed with post-traumatic stress disorder, or PTSD, due to his service during the Iraq War in 2003–2004. He is receiving treatment for his illness and taking several anti-depressant medications.

People with PTSD may relive the traumatic event that caused their condition in several ways. They may have upsetting thoughts that intrude into their daily lives or suffer from recurring nightmares. In rare cases, people with PTSD experience what are called flashbacks, vivid memories of traumatic events. A person experiencing a flashback may believe that he or she is actually reliving the event. Flashbacks can be triggered by the anniversary of the traumatic event, certain sounds, odors, or seemingly innocent activities, like children playing chase on a playground. Sometimes, the flashbacks occur with no triggers. The person experiencing the flashback can become extremely agitated and disoriented. These periods can last from a few minutes to many hours.

The news media began doing reports on PTSD and the term *flashback* in the late 1960s and early 1970s, when some soldiers returning from combat in the Vietnam War were diagnosed with the disorder and exhibited this agitated behavior. The soldiers were unable to let go of the horrors of battle and its aftermath, and the persistent thoughts affected many of them psychologically. A child crying on a playground could trigger memories of Vietnamese children crying for their dead parents. The sound of a firecracker could send soldiers mentally back to a scene of battle. Psychiatric services at veterans' facilities throughout the country have personnel trained to work with PTSD patients.

PTSD is classified as acute when the symptoms have been affecting the patient for less than three months and chronic when the symptoms have continued for more than three months. Sometimes, though, symptoms do not begin immediately after the traumatic event. Symptoms may not appear for six months, or even longer. One symptom is a drastic change in personality. For instance, a usually calm, laid-back person may become restless, irritable, or have trouble sleeping. He or she may become introverted, avoiding friends and family. If and when these symptoms appear, it is important to get help.

It is natural to try to hide weaknesses or even deny problems, altogether, but a person experiencing anxiety disorders needs to understand that this is a potentially serious mental condition, not something shameful that needs to be hidden. The person should seek help, rather than trying to hide the condition. Like the flu or any other illness, without the right kind of medical help, anxiety disorders can become much worse. Not taking the proper steps to treat these conditions can result in the loss of employment, job promotions, friendships, family relationships, and in the worst of conditions, people's lives.

CHAPTER TWO

Patient Age and Family Relationships

Anxiety disorders do not just affect the lives of the people suffering from them. They also have an impact on the lives of families and friends. These mental disorders have no social, racial, or gender barriers. Some of these disorders are more common among certain age groups, races, or genders, but the fact is, any anxiety disorder can affect anyone of any age, race, nationality, gender, or income level. They can have especially traumatic effects on the lives of children and young adults, and in very young children, anxiety disorders can be quite difficult to identify.

Anxiety Disorders Among Children and Teens

Like adults, children and teens experience stressful events in their lives that cause anxiety, but reacting to stress and anxiety does not mean that a person has an anxiety disorder. Most of the time, people can work through their worries and move on. However, some people have difficulty doing this. These are the people who may develop anxiety disorders.

Although people of any age can suffer from any form of anxiety disorder, certain types are more common among people of specific age groups. For instance, phobias, obsessive-compulsive disorder (OCD), and separation anxiety are more common in children up to age nine while general anxiety disorder (GAD), social phobia, and panic disorder appear more frequently among older children and teens. In fact, some studies indicate that 3 to 5 percent of children under eighteen have some type of anxiety disorder.

One issue, especially among young children, is that they may not be able to clearly describe how they are feeling, so it is harder for doctors to make a diagnosis. For this reason, anxiety disorders in children may be overlooked or misdiagnosed. These children may become frustrated because they cannot make people understand what they are feeling. Sometimes, their frustration causes them to act out, both at school and at home.

Separation anxiety is probably the most easily observable anxiety disorder in children. A certain amount of separation anxiety is normal when a small child's parent leaves the room for a few minutes. When children begin day care or preschool, some tears are pretty much expected, but usually the child will become interested in activities, join in, and stop crying and fretting. Some children experience these feelings quite strongly, though. These children may become extremely fearful for their parents' safety. They may be afraid something might happen to their parents, or that their parents will forget to come back and get them. In some cases, extreme homesickness can actually make them physically ill. They can suffer from headaches, stomachaches, diarrhea, nausea, even vomiting.

In addition to trying to avoid going to school, children with separation anxiety may refuse to go to parties or sleepovers. They may be excessively shy around people outside of their immediate families. In fact, they may refuse to speak to others outside the family, at all. This condition is called selective mutism. Selective mutism usually appears before five years of age and becomes especially noticeable when the child enters school or day care. Many children are extremely shy about speaking around people they do not know, but a diagnosis of this condition is

Cindy Cook sits with her six-year-old daughter Jayda, who has been diagnosed with selective mutism, a form of anxiety where a child becomes so shy she literally cannot speak.

usually not made unless the behavior has persisted for a month or more.

Young children exhibiting symptoms of separation anxiety tend to follow their parents around the house during the day. They may want a parent to stay with them until they fall asleep or try to insist that a parent sleep with them all night. They tend to awaken in the night and try to climb into bed with their parents or have nightmares about their parents going away or being lost.

Like separation anxiety, phobias are also more common among young children. Many children are afraid of the dark, especially dark rooms, the dark spaces under beds, and closets. It is fairly common for parents to make quick checks under beds and in closets to assure their young children that there are no monsters lurking. However, these fears sometimes become serious. According to one study, about 2.3 percent of children in a sample community, a community where anxiety disorders among children were studied and observed, suffered from phobic symptoms extreme enough to qualify as clinical phobic disorder. In short, many children are occasionally fearful, but if these fears trouble a child on a regular basis or appear to become more extreme, parents should consider seeking medical help.

Teenagers who isolate themselves from others and refuse to call friends may be suffering from social anxiety disorder, or SAD. These teens may eventually turn to drugs or alcohol to cope with their feelings of low self esteem.

One of the anxiety disorders that tends to affect older children and teens is GAD. As with adults, GAD is characterized by excessive worry and anxiety about many different things. For young people, these worries revolve around such issues as grades; their performance in sports, music, or plays; being on time for classes and clubs; family problems; their health; and the weather, as well as other issues.

Young people with GAD suffer from physical symptoms such as irritability, fatigue, insomnia, restlessness, and general muscle tension. These children tend to be perfectionists. They may redo school reports or projects several times and still not be satisfied with their work. They constantly seek approval from others and are often very hard on themselves.

Another anxiety disorder that affects teens is social anxiety disorder (SAD). SAD is the intense fear of social situations. Teens with SAD have difficulty engaging others in conversation, speaking in front of their classes, organizing get-togethers with friends, or doing any sort of performances before groups, like class plays, skits, debating, or singing. This condition affects the quality of young people's school experiences as well as personal relationships.

Young people with SAD are often seen sitting alone in the library or cafeteria. They avoid eye contact and mumble or speak very softly. They will seldom call friends on the telephone or get with classmates to work on homework or projects. They are, basically, loners who isolate themselves from others. If asked, young people with this condition would probably admit to being unhappy with their lives. They feel as though they are on the outside, looking in. As with other anxiety disorders, young people who suffer from SAD may become involved with drugs and alcohol and tend to have low self-esteem.

Panic disorder generally occurs among older teens. These young people experience sudden periods of extreme irrational fear. This fear is accompanied by some physical symptoms that may be the same as those suffered by adults and some that may be different. Symptoms described by some young people include nausea; trembling; a feeling of "going crazy;"

Even Among the Very Powerful

Obsessive-compulsive disorder (OCD) knows no boundaries. Texas-born aviator, engineer, industrialist, and motion-picture producer-director Howard Hughes was enormously talented and fabulously wealthy. He was born to wealth, but also accumulated a fortune on his own. Despite his distinguished career and many successes, though, Hughes may be best known for the symptoms of OCD that plagued him for many years of his life.

Some friends remarked that Hughes was obsessed with certain foods, especially peas. He would sort them by size and eat them with a special fork. During his years in the film industry, colleagues reported that he would become obsessed over minor details, such as the fit of actress Jane Russell's blouse, in the movie, *The Outlaw*. Hughes was said to have written a lengthy description of how to repair the offending garment.

Symptoms of OCD manifested in other ways, as well. In his professional life, he became obsessed with owning Texas-founded hotels and restaurants. Personally, he became morbidly fearful of germs and dirt. In his later years, he would not shake hands with anyone and often engaged in hand-washing rituals. He would also get stuck on certain phrases and repeat them, over and over.

He became so obsessed and fearful that, by the time of his death in April 1976, he was no longer recognizable. His 6-foot, (1.8m) 4-inch (10cm), malnourished frame had withered to only 90 pounds (41km). His hair, as well as his fingernails and toenails, had gone untrimmed for years. In fact, his remains were so unrecognizable that the FBI had to identify him through his fingerprints.

a feeling of things being unreal, like being in a dream; and a need to escape.

Under the best of conditions, the teen years can be difficult. No teenager wants to be strange or different. Many young people have not yet developed a strong sense of self-worth or self-confidence. Additionally, teens dread doing anything other teens would find socially unacceptable. Peer acceptance is one of the top teen priorities, and overly active hormones can result in crying jags or temper eruptions over relatively minor issues. When an anxiety disorder is added to this mix, the results can be devastating and can have lasting effects on a young person's life. If any sort of disorder is suspected, the sooner the young person receives the proper attention, the better chances of a full recovery and a successful, rewarding future.

Anxiety Disorders in Adults

Some anxiety disorders are more common among adults than children. Furthermore, according to some studies, certain anxiety disorders tend to affect people of some races and cultures more so than others. For instance, one study determined that more African Americans are affected by phobias than are people of other races. Additionally, some countries have their own individual forms of anxiety disorders. For example, in Japan there is a recognized form of social phobia called *taijin kyofusho*. People with this disorder fear that their appearance, odor, or even their faces are offensive to others. Latin America even has its own anxiety disorder called *nervious*, or nerves. Latin Americans suffering from this condition experience insomnia, headaches, and dizziness. Most Latin cultures are very family oriented, and this high degree of family devotion is the basis of this condition. *Nervious* is often linked to the loss of a close friend or relative or to family conflict.

Finally, between the genders, various studies indicate that at least twice as many women are affected by anxiety disorders than are men. Some researchers believe this is because women tend to worry more than men. For example, women are twice as likely to suffer from GAD. However, some professionals believe that more men than women suffer from post-traumatic stress disorder (PTSD), because men traditionally hold the

Research has shown that biological, social, and psychological factors may cause women to be more anxious than men.

high-risk jobs that can result in severe psychological trauma, such as active-duty soldiers, firefighters, and police officers. Women with PTSD are more frequently victims of physical violence and psychological trauma than are men.

Additionally, more women than men suffer from specific phobias, panic disorder, and agoraphobia. Men and women are about equal with regard to social phobia; however, some studies put the numbers slightly higher among men. Finally, most studies conclude that the numbers of men and women diagnosed with OCD are about equal.

Some research indicates that certain biological, social, and psychological factors may also make some women more prone to anxiety. According to this research, some of the blame can be placed on female hormones. Supposedly, changes in women's reproductive hormones can make them feel more vulnerable and anxious. Specifically, this can occur when a woman's estrogen and progesterone levels are low. Addi-

Do I Have an Anxiety Disorder?

Just because someone feels anxious at times, does not mean the person has an anxiety disorder. However, certain feelings and symptoms might indicate the need for professional help. Feeling frequently restless, distracted, or irritable could be early warning signs of an anxiety disorder. Chronically tense muscles, sometimes described as a feeling of knots in the muscles, often go along with these feelings. If a person has more sleepless nights than restful ones, this could be another symptom. More severe symptoms include repeating the same phrase over and over; counting, checking or washing rituals; unreasonable fear of objects or situations; and excessive worrying. Sometimes, younger people are not comfortable discussing these issues with parents or other family members. If this is the case, students can talk with a school counselor.

tionally, according to traditional beliefs, women, as a whole, are less assertive than men, and this makes them more susceptible to stress. Others believe that women are more likely to express fears than men or perhaps that it is more acceptable in American society for women to show anxiety and fear than men.

Regarding the cultural issue, some studies conclude that women are more likely to fear embarrassment and humiliation caused by making mistakes in their jobs than are men. Women fear being seen as incompetent. This might lead some women to retreat from high-risk or management positions to jobs where they feel safer.

Men, on the other hand, have specific issues of their own when it comes to anxiety disorders. For one thing, men, on the whole, are less likely to seek medical or psychological help when they have problems that affect their mental or physical health. This may be because, regardless of culture or race, most men do not want to appear weak in any way. They associate anxiety disorders with emotional problems, and emotional issues are often considered women's problems. In fact, some men who suffer from panic disorder turn to alcohol to dull the symptoms. Others go further, retreating into both alcohol and drug abuse. In a study of men and women with agoraphobia, which often accompanies panic disorder, nearly twice as many men as women are alcoholics. This can jeopardize and eventually destroy careers, friendships, and families.

Another problem men with anxiety disorders experience is misdiagnosis, especially with panic disorder because some of the symptoms of panic disorder are similar to those of physical problems. Because of this, panic disorder, especially in men, may be misdiagnosed as possible heart attack, cardiac arrhythmia, thyroid problems, or even epilepsy.

Anxiety Disorders in the Elderly

At one time, it was believed that the tendency to have anxiety disorders decreased as people approached their later years. Some experts now believe that older men and women are less likely than young people to seek help for psychiatric problems. Additionally, older people tend to focus on their physical problems, rather than mental ones. The fact is, though, that about 20 percent of all elderly people experience symptoms of anxiety.

According to the Anxiety Disorders Association of America, "until recently, anxiety disorders were believed to decline with age. But now experts are beginning to recognize that aging and anxiety are not mutually exclusive: anxiety is as common in the old as in the young, although how and when it appears is distinctly different in older adults."[7]

Since experts have begun to realize that anxiety is a mental health issue among the old as well as the young, they have made a number of connections. Researchers have determined that younger and older people have several issues in common when it comes to anxiety disorders. They are more common among women than among men. Anxiety and depression are as closely linked in older people as they are in younger people.

An elderly man stands among the many possessions he has hoarded over the years. Hoarding is the most common type of obsessive-compulsive disorder among elderly people.

Another trait the elderly share with young people is that there are more anxiety disorders among people of both age groups who have less formal education. Although this is a shared trait, the reason behind it is not known.

Dr. Gene Cohen described another similarity between young children and cognitively impaired older adults, such as people with Alzheimer's disease. Being cognitively impaired can make diagnosing anxiety disorders especially difficult: "Both [a young child and the cognitively impaired] may have a limited capacity to tell you how they feel . . . but there are many examples in the case of anxiety where the diagnosis does not rely on what patients say, but rather what they display."[8]

Many older people with anxiety disorders had at least one or more of these conditions when they were young, and may have overcome them. Older people face many stressful situations as they age. These include the loss of spouses, friends, and family; problems with physical health; limited money; and memory problems. All too often, an older person is dealing with two or more of these serious issues at the same time, which can be emotionally overwhelming. If these people are retired with lots of spare time on their hands and few productive activities to occupy their minds, they can become totally preoccupied with the stressful issues in their lives. This can trigger the return of their earlier anxiety disorders. When these anxiety disorders are combined with their other problems, older people can become mentally and physically exhausted, which disrupts their daily lives and can further damage their health.

With stressful issues coming at them from a variety of sources, elderly people sometimes feel that they are being hit from every direction at once. Because of this, the most common anxiety disorder among the elderly is GAD. In fact, one in thirty older people suffers from GAD.

Two other anxiety disorders that tend to affect older people are OCD and phobic disorders. Many older people experience different types of phobic disorders. The most common type of phobia among older people is fear of falling. This can be an especially significant fear among older people who live alone.

They worry about how they can get help if they fall and cannot get to a telephone.

Other phobias center around airplanes, heights, storms, and illness. Some older people also develop social phobias and fear going out in public and being around groups of people. As with anxiety disorders among younger people, about twice as many elderly women as men are affected by phobias.

The most common type of OCD among the elderly is hoarding. The most serious hoarders are usually people over the age of sixty. This is because the problem often begins with clutter, which is messy and can be a nuisance. However, the compulsion to gather increases over the years to the point that the person's home is a safety as well as a health hazard. When the situation reaches this point, it is hoarding. Older hoarders may isolate themselves from family and friends, ashamed to have people see their homes, but seemingly powerless to do anything about it. These people are unable to make decisions. They cannot choose what to discard and what to keep. Not only is this a serious issue for the hoarder, but also for the children or grandchildren of the hoarder, who will ultimately have to deal with the rooms full of old newspapers, plastic containers, used aluminum foil, and other piles of objects, as well as the vermin that may be hiding among the piles of litter. The situation might be so severe that the family will have to hire a special cleaning service and also deal with an irate and indignant parent or grandparent who seriously resents what seems like an intrusion into his or her privacy. This hoarding sometimes extends to animals. There are many documented cases of animal control agencies removing dozens of dogs and cats from homes of elderly people. The conditions in these homes are usually serious health hazards to both the animals and the humans.

Family, Friends, and Environmental Factors

Whatever the age of the person with the anxiety disorder, family members and friends face a variety of challenges. Some of these challenges can be quite serious. One problem is isolation.

Children who have parents suffering with anxiety disorders may feel different from or inferior to other children and as a result isolate themselves from classmates and neighbors.

Often, the person suffering from the anxiety disorder becomes socially isolated; however, this isolation can carry over into the family, as well.

For instance, the mother may have panic attacks, which forces the rest of the family to turn down invitations to parties, weddings, or other social events. Parents with social disorders may not be able to attend their children's recitals, plays, or sporting events, which can result in the children quitting these activities. They see classmates' parents in the audience or the bleachers, cheering on their children and supporting them in their activities. If their own parents are not supportive, the children who have parents with these disorders may feel that they are different or inferior and may quit participating in the activities they once enjoyed.

It is natural for family, friends, and neighbors to wonder if something is wrong if the family suddenly becomes socially isolated. This is especially true if there are children in the family, and they are no longer seen at the community pool, park, or even playing in their own yards. If the mother quits going to the local grocery store or stops attending school meetings and events, this can also trigger suspicion. Deciding who to be open with about family problems, such as anxiety disorders, is a tough call. However, there is usually some friend or relative with whom family members can discuss their concerns; someone who can discretely reassure neighbors that the family is just going through a difficult time. No one is being mistreated. Such a confidant can be helpful in preventing well-meaning neighbors from possibly overreacting by calling Children's Protective Services or some other agency.

In addition to problems and reactions outside the family, household routines and responsibilities can become disrupted. If a parent is seriously affected by an anxiety disorder, depending on the disorder, the other parent may have to take on all of the household and parenting chores. The list can be quite extensive, such as making sure all of the bills are paid on time, doing the grocery shopping, getting the children to and from school and other activities, and doing all of the cooking and cleaning, in addition to working a full-time job. The partner taking up all of the slack can become overwhelmed, exhausted, and burned out. Because of this, in some instances, the parent with all of the responsibilities may seek a more stable, normal relationship outside the marriage, while still attending to all of the household duties. On the other hand, this person might also physically walk away from the marriage.

One parent's anxiety disorder can also have a financial affect on the family. If this parent has been contributing financially to the family's welfare and becomes so involved in the condition that he or she loses a job, this dumps the entire financial responsibility onto the other parent. With so many households relying on two-parent incomes, the results can be financially devastating. At the very least, luxuries have to go. At the worst, the family might lose its home or have to move in with friends or family for a while or into a smaller, less expensive place.

When a child has an anxiety disorder, some parents might first think it is a phase, just some part of childhood that their son or daughter will outgrow. In the beginning, they may ignore or rationalize the outward symptoms of the disorder. Some parents feel guilty, wondering if they are doing something to cause the child's problem. These parents may go along with the behavior, treating it as normal and acceptable. By adapting the home environment to the disorder, trying to make things "easier" for the child, even expecting siblings to go along with the behavior, the parents and siblings become codependent. They make themselves part of the problem, rather than seeking help and working toward a solution. Over time, if the behaviors continue, one or both of the parents, as well as the siblings, may become angry or impatient. They may think the child is just acting out to get attention. They may think the child should just snap out of it, but people do not "snap out" of anxiety disorders. As with any other health problem, children and adults with anxiety disorders usually do not recover or improve without the proper treatment.

CHAPTER THREE

Diagnosis and Treatment

Anxiety disorders are the most common of all mental disorders. Because they are so common, it might seem that anxiety disorders would be the easiest mental problems to diagnose and treat. This is not the case, though. Many people with anxiety disorders are receiving little treatment, no treatment, or perhaps even the wrong kind of treatment. There are a number of reasons for this. First, some people are unaware that they have an anxiety disorder. They may think it is simply a peculiar quirk of their personality, and they choose to live with it the best way they can. Others are aware they have a problem, but choose to ignore it, perhaps thinking the problem will fix itself, or that admitting that they have a psychological problem is something shameful or makes them appear weak. Still others are aware they have a problem, but think it has something to do with their physical health. They may visit their family physicians, have tests run, and still not receive the correct diagnosis. This is not necessarily a failing on the part of physicians, but rather the fact that some of the symptoms of anxiety disorders are the same as those of some physical conditions, such as heart problems. In fact, if left untreated, anxiety disorders can have a negative affect on a person's physical health. Insomnia or eating problems may develop, for example. However, once a correct diagnosis is made and appropriate treatment given, a person's chances of recovery from an anxiety disorder are actually quite high.

Interviews, Written Evaluations, and Medical Testing

As with any type of illness, the first steps toward recovery are seeking help and being diagnosed correctly. The diagnostic process for anxiety disorders requires several different types of procedures. This process can be quite tricky, because anxiety is a symptom of so many different disorders. In addition to anxiety disorders, anxiety is also a symptom of depression and schizophrenia, a mental disorder characterized by delusions and hallucinations. Anxiety can also result from physical conditions, like diseases of the brain, some types of heart disease, and hyperglycemia, which is an abnormally high amount of sugar in the blood, often associated with diabetes. Even the patient's diet needs to be evaluated for foods and drink high in caffeine, which can also produce symptoms of anxiety.

Since anxiety can be caused by so many different conditions, both physical and mental, doctors are very thorough in their evaluations. They need to know the patient's medical history, a general medical history of close family members to determine if any anxiety-related conditions run in the family, and have a complete list of medications the patient is currently taking. Additionally, the patient, and frequently the patient's family, will be interviewed by psychiatric specialists. This part of the diagnostic process usually consists of interviews, several short-answer questionnaires, as well as symptom inventories. Among these evaluations are the Hamilton Anxiety Scale (HAMA) and the Anxiety Disorders Interview Schedule (ADIS).

The HAMA is a questionnaire with a built-in rating scale. Each of the fourteen topics, such as fears, tension, and anxious moods, has a rating ranging from zero, for not present, to four, for severe. Patients choose the rating for each topic that best describes themselves. The ADIS is a structured inter-

A patient should have a through medical evaluation with his doctor to help determine the cause of his anxiety disorder and the best way to treat it.

view to determine a patient's current feelings of anxiety and to diagnose which anxiety disorder or disorders the patient is presently experiencing. Additionally, it contains a section on family psychiatric history and helps determine whether or not the anxiety problem is tied to substance abuse. There are both an adult's version and a two-part, parent-and-child version for young patients.

In addition to psychological evaluations, the patient may also be tested to determine if the anxiety problems are linked to any physical conditions. For instance, since anxiety can also be a symptom of brain tumors, physicians may elect to run noninvasive tests, such as a magnetic resonance imaging (MRI), which can create a three-dimensional image of the brain; a computerized axial tomography (CT scan), which creates an X-ray image of the brain; or an electroencephalogram (EEG), which is a record of the electrical activity of the brain. Finally, heart disease can be ruled out with an electrocardiogram (ECG). This device measures the electrical currents associated with heart function.

Extreme anxiety is also a symptom of blood sugar and thyroid problems, so the patient will probably have laboratory tests, as well. Both the patient's blood and urine are tested. These tests include a complete blood count (CBC), which determines the quantity of each type of blood cell present in a sample of blood, and a chemistry profile, a group of tests performed on a blood sample. Thyroid function tests determine how well the thyroid, a large gland in the neck, is secreting the hormones which influence growth and metabolism. Additionally, one or two tests will probably be performed on a urine sample. These tests are a urinalysis, which provides an indication of general health, especially kidney function, and a drug screen, to determine which, if any, drugs are present in the body.

As with the diagnostic process for any disease or condition, these procedures take time. There is no such thing as an instant diagnosis. When the physicians and mental health specialists have had time to gather and evaluate all of the data, they will have all of the relevant facts at hand to make the best

Strokes and Anxiety

A stroke is a hemorrhage of a blood vessel leading to the brain. This event can result in difficulty speaking as well as weakness or paralysis of the arms, legs, and even the face. For years, the medical community has recognized that many stroke patients experience bouts of depression. Recent studies, though, are finding connections between stroke and anxiety disorders. For instance, one study reported an increase in both agoraphobia and generalized anxiety disorder (GAD) among patients following stroke. Another study found GAD in 24 percent of patients with acute stroke. Patients usually develop these anxiety disorders at periods of time ranging from three months to three years following their stroke.

diagnosis for the patient. At this time, the medical team will work with the patient to determine the best course of treatment. Among the options is psychotherapy or psychotherapy with medication.

Psychotherapy

Psychotherapy is an approach to treating mental disorders using psychiatry, psychology, or both. A large part of psychotherapy involves verbal communication. The appropriate type of psychotherapy chosen for the patient is supervised by therapists with special training in specific areas of psychiatry or psychology. Psychotherapy's effectiveness as a treatment tool is described by Dr. John March of the Department of Psychiatry at the Duke University Medical Center in Durham, North Carolina: "Medication . . . is effective to get an immediate reduction of symptoms. However, its effects only last as long as the patient takes the drug. Research shows that combination therapies or CBT (cognitive-behavior therapy) alone have longer lasting effects and help prevent relapse."[9]

Three elderly women and a therapist participating in art therapy, a form of treatment used to help people cope with certain traumatic experiences.

Psychotherapy is not one type of treatment but many. These include art therapy, behavior therapy, cognitive therapy, cognitive-behavior therapy, exposure therapy, and psychoanalysis, among others. A prescribed course of psychotherapy can be short term, requiring just a few visits with a qualified therapist. More likely, though, it will continue for a longer period of time, even up to a number of years. Psychotherapy sessions might involve one person, couples, or even entire families, depending on the patient's need.

Art therapy, or creative art therapy, helps people who have difficulty expressing themselves in words. In addition to drawing or painting, creative art therapy includes drama, music, poetry, and even dance. This type of therapy can help people cope with certain traumatic experiences. This is especially true of children who have been traumatized by family violence. Younger children may not have sufficient vocabulary to express their feelings, but they can draw them or act them out. This not only helps the children express their feelings, but also gives therapists a clearer picture of the types of trauma the children have experienced.

The next type of therapy, behavior therapy, helps the patient change unwanted, unhealthy, or inappropriate behaviors. This usually involves reinforcements or rewards for positive behavior and desensitization. The process of desensitization involves confronting or exposing oneself to the object, place, or event that causes anxiety or fear and overcoming those feelings. For instance, if a person has difficulty speaking in public, that person will first be exposed to lower-anxiety situations that require speaking before a few people, and then to more anxiety-causing situations with the final goal being that the person is comfortable speaking before large groups of people.

Cognitive therapy deals exclusively with whatever problem the patient is currently experiencing. This type of therapy does not deal with problems, issues, or conflicts from the person's past. The purpose of cognitive therapy is to modify inappropriate, disturbing, or destructive thought patterns. The patient and the therapist work to change the way the patient sees himself or herself. This, in turn, helps the patient change self-destructive or other inappropriate behavior.

Cognitive-behavior therapy is a combination of cognitive and behavior therapies. This type of therapy is based on the premise that people's own ideas, rather than situations or the actions of others, determine the way they think and behave. For instance, if a situation, such as a stressful job, is not likely to change, the person can learn to change the way he or she thinks and behaves in the job setting, and begin responding in more positive ways.

Exposure therapy is actually a form of behavior therapy. The patient is repeatedly exposed to the place, object, person, or situation that causes the anxiety. This form of therapy is especially helpful to people with post-traumatic stress disorder (PTSD) or obsessive-compulsive disorder (OCD). According to the beliefs of experts who use this type of therapy in treating their patients, constant exposure to the objects or events that cause the anxiety or obsessive thoughts or behavior will help the patient learn to control them.

The final example of psychotherapy is psychoanalysis. In psychoanalysis, therapists help patients examine feelings, experiences, and events from their pasts. By doing this, the patients can come to understand how the past influences current feelings, compulsions, and other behaviors. Psychoanalysis might include dream analysis, talking about a patient's recurring dreams, or a process called free association, discussing whatever randomly comes to the patient's mind. Developed from the theories of Austrian neurologist and psychiatrist, Sigmund Freud, psychoanalysis is a long-term process. In fact, this course of treatment could involve two or more sessions a week for several years.

Medications

Once the diagnostic process is complete, one option the physician has is choosing medication from the groups of drugs that have been developed for use in the treatment of mental disorders. Med-

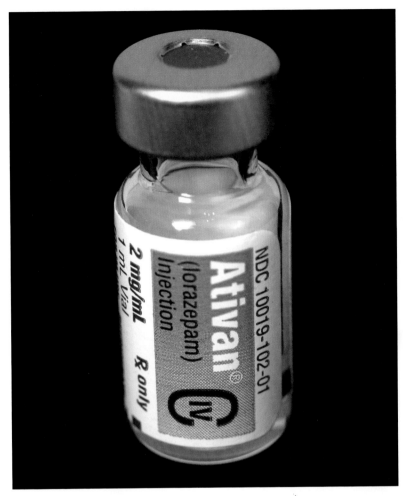

Although commonly given to anxiety patients in the past, benzodiazepine drugs, such as Ativan, are now only given to patients who have extreme cases of anxiety disorders.

ication is usually prescribed if the anxiety symptoms are serious to the point that they interfere with the patient's daily life. These drug groups include selective serotonin reuptake inhibitors, tricyclic antidepressants, benzodiazepines, monoamine oxadase inhibitors, and even antihistamines. These drug groups act in the body in different ways to treat symptoms of anxiety disorders.

For quite some time, the group most commonly prescribed for symptoms of anxiety disorders is benzodiazepines. Now, though, doctors limit the use of this group of drugs to the most severe cases of anxiety. Benzodiazepines work by depressing the part of the brain that regulates brain activity. This group of drugs can be given orally, or in extreme cases when the patient needs to be sedated, it can be given intravenously, through a vein. Diazepam (Valium) and lorazepam (Ativan) are the two most commonly prescribed benzodiazepines. Of the two, lorazepam is effective longer, but it takes longer for the effects to begin. As with other drug groups, though, benzodiazepines can have side effects. For example, if taken longer than a few weeks, the patient can become both physically and psychologically dependent upon and addicted to the drugs. Their body has become used to, or tolerant, of the drugs and this means that, in order to produce the same results, the patient will need stronger and stronger doses. When someone has developed an addiction to any drug, either prescribed or illegal, the person has to go through an uncomfortable and difficult time called withdrawal in order to break free of the drug. Symptoms of benzodiazepine withdrawal syndrome include confusion, loss of appetite, shaking, sweating, insomnia, and ringing in the ears. Because of the danger of patients becoming addicted to benzodiazepines, many doctors do not prescribe them for longer than four weeks, and use it only for the most extreme cases.

Due to the problems with how long the benzodiazepines can be used for a course of treatment, some doctors determine that triclyic antidepressants (TCAs) are relatively safer for their patients. One reason these drugs are sometimes chosen over benzodiazepines is that they can be given to patients over a

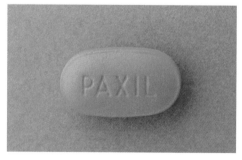

Paxil is from a group of antidepressants known as selective serotonin reuptake inhibitors (SSRIs) and is one of the most commonly prescribed drugs for people with anxiety disorders.

longer period of time with less chance of the patients building a tolerance and becoming addicted. Named for the three rings of atoms in their molecular structure, TCAs have been around since the 1950s. They work by helping two neurotransmitters, norepinepherine and serotonin, work effectively in the brain. These two neurotransmitters work as chemical messengers, sending "feel good" messages to the brain. The TCAs help keep these chemical messengers active by preventing them from being reabsorbed. Among several of these antidepressants are amitriptyline (Elavil) and amoxapine (Moxadil).

Like the benzodiazepines, TCAs have some side effects. Side effects include dry mouth and nose, difficulty with urination, irregular heartbeat, blurred vision, dizziness, and drowsiness. If a patient is experiencing any of the last three side effects, driving and operating machinery could be dangerous.

Selective serotonin reuptake inhibitors (SSRIs) were developed more recently than TCAs and are now the most commonly prescribed group of antidepressants. Like TCAs, SSRIs act on the serotonin in the brain. SSRIs include sertraline (Zoloft), paroxetine (Paxil), and fluoxetine (Prozac).

Most of the drugs in this group are not suitable for children or teens under the age of eighteen because they are too powerful for bodies that are still growing and developing. They also carry the potential for problems in adults sixty-five and over. Older people taking these drugs may become dizzy and are more likely to fall, causing fractures and other injuries. This group of drugs carries the risk of psychological symptoms, such as increased anxiety, agitated behavior, and increased hostility. Other side effects include insomnia, nausea, dry mouth, dizziness, drowsiness, fatigue, and headaches. There is also a risk of withdrawal symptoms if a person stops taking this type of drug without consulting their doctor. Patients must be weaned off the drug by taking smaller and smaller doses over a period of time.

A fourth group of drugs used in the treatment of anxiety disorders is monoamine oxidase inhibitors (MAOIs). Earlier MAOIs were used only as a last resort, but some of the newer drugs in this group are now being used as a first-line treatment. MAOIs prevent monoamine oxidase, a liver and brain enzyme, from doing its clean-up job. Monoamine oxidase burns up neurotransmitters, serotonin, norepinephrine, and dopamine, once they have done their part in transmitting messages to the brain. If monoamine oxidase is prevented from doing its job, the neurotransmitters build up. This results in lowering anxiety and easing depression. Side effects patients may experience from MAOIs include dizziness, drowsiness, and blurred vision. MAOIs also require some dietary restrictions. Patients cannot eat cheeses, pickled foods, or chocolates or drink alcoholic or non-alcoholic beers or wines because a substance called tryamine

Treating Anxiety Disorders with Homeopathy

Homeopathy is a form of alternative and complementary medicine. Part of the homeopathic approach is controversial, though. According to the principals of homeopathy, certain substances can cause symptoms of illness in the body, but when diluted, these substances that produce the symptoms can actually aid the patient in recovering from the illness. For example, two substances, arsenicum album (arsenic) and nux vomica (poison nut) might be administered in diluted form to treat anxiety. The choice of drug administered would depend on physical traits, personality, and behavior of the patient.

Other aspects of homeopathy are generally accepted, however, such as counseling on nutrition, stress management, and exercise. Additionally, the goal of homeopathy is to treat the underlying cause of anxiety, not just the symptoms. While homeopathy is a choice of treatment, no medical procedure should be ended or begun without the knowledge and support of the physician in charge of the patient's case.

will flood the brain. This substance causes the blood pressure to rise. When MAOIs keep monoamine oxidase from doing its job, one of the other substances it cannot mop up is the tryamine. Excessive amounts of tryamine can actually cause blood pressure to rise so severely that blood vessels can burst in the brain. Three common types of MAOIs are phenelzine (Nardil), tranylcypromine (Parnate), and isocarboxazid (Marplan).

Because of the potential severity of the side effects, one psychiatrist, Andy Myerson, describes the conditions in which he would use the earlier drugs of this group: "I call it the 'St. Jude' drug. It's the drug I use when nothing else works and someone is willing to give up anything in the hope that something will help their depression."[10]

Another group of drugs sometimes used to treat anxiety disorders are antihistamines. More commonly associated with the treatment of allergies, antihistamines block histamine, which is another neurotransmitter. Antihistamines work quickly, producing a sedating effect. However, antihistamines have some side effects and other potential problems, as well. Too high a dose can impair psychomotor skills, which is a sequence of task-oriented steps involving eye-hand coordination, and patients can develop a mild tolerance. Side effects include weakness, problems with concentration, frequent urination, and heart palpitations.

Basically, all of the drugs discussed here have potential benefits as well as possible side effects. To lessen the chances of adverse reactions, patients should carefully follow their doctors' orders and the directions that come with the prescriptions. If they notice any side effects, they should contact their doctors immediately.

Alternative Therapies

The path to recovery for patients is not limited to psychotherapy and medications. In some instances, alternative therapies have proven successful in relieving anxiety. Some people use these forms of therapy in conjunction with more conventional therapies while others try to rely on alternative therapies,

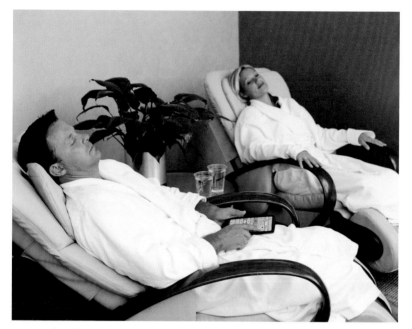

A couple relaxing in message chairs. Research has shown that massage therapy can reduce stress and, in turn, lessen anxiety.

alone. These alternative therapies include massage, aroma-therapy, vitamin supplements, and diet.

Massage therapy has been shown to lower anxiety and stress and decrease the hormones that cause stress. In a study conducted at the Touch Research Institute at the University of Miami School of Medicine, one group of subjects was given chair massage twice a week for five weeks. The control group, the group of people who did not receive massage, was directed to simply relax in the massage chairs for fifteen minutes. Both groups were monitored by means of EEGs before, during, and following the study period and were rated on several psychological scales prior to and after the study period. In addition to a marked lowering of anxiety levels, the group receiving the massage showed enhanced alertness and increased speed and accuracy in math skills over the control group. In conclusion, this study indicates that massage therapy benefits people not only by relieving anxiety, but also by improving mental alertness.

Aromatherapy also appears to benefit some people by lowering anxiety. According to aromatherapists, using certain fragrant substances in lotions and inhalants can improve mood and overall general health. These practitioners believe that people who have anxiety disorders are extra sensitive to changes within their own bodies, which raises anxiety. They believe that the use of these products can enhance the beneficial effects of other types of treatment by helping the patient relax.

A number of studies have determined that anxiety can also be relieved by making adjustments in diet. According to research, stimulants, salt, preservatives, hormones in meat, and refined sweets can elevate anxiety. Among the worst dietary offenders are stimulants such as caffeinated products like coffee, tea, and colas, and alcohol. These substances can interrupt sleep and increase nervousness and anxiety. They do this by depleting the body of the natural vitamins and minerals that help keep moods in balance. Salt can cause problems in the diet also. It takes calcium out of the body. Calcium is important in the function of the central nervous system. Additionally, salt causes a rise in blood pressure, which puts a strain on the arteries and the heart.

Preservatives in commercially prepared foods can also increase the symptoms of anxiety disorders. The human body is not designed to process the more than five thousand chemical additives currently used in commercial food processing. At this time, there is little investigation being done to examine exactly what long- and short-term effects these substances have on the mind and body. This being the case, it is best to avoid processed foods as much as possible. There are similar questions about the hormones that are being fed to cattle, hogs, and poultry in order to increase the amount of meat that can be harvested from these animals. Finally, sweets affect the blood sugar, which can cause mood swings and elevate anxiety. The safest course to follow for a person who is trying to control anxiety by diet is to cut down on foods with these substances in them.

In addition to the types of foods that patients eat, the way they consume food is also important. A number of bad habits can cause digestive problems, which in turn causes stress. Eating too fast, eating on the run, and eating too much at one time can cause indigestion and cramping. Bad eating habits put a strain on the digestive system which can prevent proper digestion from taking place and can keep the body from absorbing essential nutrients that decrease anxiety. Therefore, decreasing substances that can harm the diet while increasing fresh and organically grown foods and setting aside ample, uninterrupted time for meals can have a beneficial effect on a person's physical and mental well-being.

Benefits of Exercise

Exercise is good for the body in a variety of ways. In addition to improving the function of the cardiovascular and respiratory systems and helping a person lose weight, exercise is good for

The practice of yoga has been determined to be a beneficial way to treat anxiety disorders by relaxing the body and alleviating stress and tension.

mental health. The brain and the body react chemically to exercise, which contributes to an overall feeling of relaxation. In fact, when someone exercises, the body generates the production of substances, such as serotonin and endorphins which send calming messages to the brain. While serotonin sends chemical "feel good" messages to the brain, endorphins act as natural painkillers in the body. Together, these substances lower stress and anxiety and cause a feeling of well-being. Just thirty to forty minutes of aerobic exercise three or four times a week stimulates the body's production of these chemicals. The exercise can be walking, jogging, bicycling, playing tennis, aerobics, or swimming. Exercise reduces muscle tension, one effect of stress and anxiety. Exercise is also a healthy outlet for the "fight or flight" state of mind caused by anxiety. In addition to raising stress-lowering hormones, exercise also reduces chemicals in the body that increase stress.

One type of exercise that some people find especially helpful in relieving stress and anxiety is yoga. Yoga is a combination of breathing exercises, postures, and meditation that are practiced in order to achieve control over the body and the mind. Shallow breathing is associated with anxiety and panic attacks. With yoga, a person can learn breathing techniques that help achieve relaxation and a sense of calm. The yoga postures stretch the muscles, relieving tension and relaxing the body, and meditation calms and focuses the mind, which also helps relieve stress.

Probably, no one type of therapy will totally rid a person of anxiety disorders or help manage the symptoms. A combination of therapies may be more effective. Additionally, patients must realize that there are no quick fixes for anxiety disorders. However, the proper therapies and possibly some lifestyle changes will greatly increase a person's chances of successfully achieving and maintaining control over anxiety disorders.

CHAPTER FOUR

Coping with Anxiety and Anxiety Disorders

Patients and their families would no doubt be relieved and grateful if someone would develop an immediate cure, a pill or some other fast-acting therapy, for anxiety disorders. At this time, however, there is no one pill, capsule, or one-time treatment that will fix anxiety disorders instantly, nor are there any instant cures currently being researched. The fact is that the treatment and recovery process for anxiety disorders or any type of mental disorder is usually long term and ongoing. Because of this, a person undergoing treatment for anxiety disorders faces a number of challenges during this time of treatment, whatever the duration. These include how strangers may react should the person's anxiety disorder erupt in some bizarre behavior while the person is in a public place; the person's own self-esteem issues resulting from years of stressful episodes, and the turmoil and stress the disorder has caused within his or her own family. This is not to say that patients and their families are helpless, though. In fact, there are several ways patients and their family members can help themselves during the recovery process, while patients are undergoing treatment.

Specific Coping Skills

Challenges of daily life can cause stress and anxiety. These stressors can range from issues as serious as threats of terrorism, catastrophic weather, and the general safety and welfare of one's family members, to relationships, jobs, and money problems. Whatever the issue, there are a variety of self-help tools to help cope with them. One of these is a five-step exercise.

Step one is to identify the specific issue that is causing the stress. This might be a job interview, a final exam, a person, or the death of a close friend or family member. The second step is to identify all personal thoughts related to the stressful situation. These thoughts may be realistic and based on facts or irrational, based on fears. The next step is focusing on the negative thoughts and reactions. Physical responses might be a stiff neck, headache, upset stomach, or loss of sleep. Emotional reactions could be nervousness, severe

Daily life, such as job pressures, can cause stress and anxiety. It is important to develop coping mechanisms to help deal with this tension.

depression, anger, or feelings of guilt. Behavioral reactions may include binge eating, avoiding people, or avoiding the issue that is causing the stress. The fourth step involves confronting the negative responses and seeing them for what they are: self-defeating. This can be difficult, because these negative responses may have been influencing the person's life for so long a time that they have become habit. These may include self put-downs, over-generalizing thoughts like "things are awful now and they'll probably stay that way forever," and all-or-nothing thinking, such as "if I don't make a good grade on this test I am an utter failure." Other negative responses are the tendency to jump to negative conclusions, mistaking feelings for facts, or converting positives into negatives, such as "sure I made a good grade on this test, but that will make it so much worse if I fail the next one." The final step is to replace the negative or inaccurate ideas with positive, accurate ones. This, too, can be difficult, because spontaneous negative thoughts are hard to control. One way to turn around negative thoughts is to compose a positive thought and let it replay in the mind like a recording. Another way to change thoughts and beliefs is to accept the fact that everyone makes mistakes. Despite best efforts, people do backslide once in a while. It is important to remember that these things do not make someone a bad or worthless person, or a failure. It is also important to focus on successes, even the small ones. For instance, if a person makes it from breakfast to lunch without having a compulsive thought or behavior, this is a success. Going all day without obsessing about fears is a major achievement and this is one of those times when self-praise is a good thing. Some situations are harder than others to put these efforts into practice, but these steps are like taking piano lessons. Skills improve with practice.

A person coping with anxiety disorders should set goals, but these goals should be realistic. For instance, a hoarder probably cannot suddenly decide to clear a room of debris when the overflowing room has been months or years in the making. The person might begin by clearing a corner, a

A compulsive hand washer may set a realistic goal of cutting his or her hand washing in half as a way of coping with obsessive-compulsive disorder.

pathway, or perhaps by taking all of the old newspapers and magazines cluttering the room to a recycle bin. A compulsive hand washer, someone who washes his or her hands six or seven times in a row before each meal, might begin by consciously cutting that compulsive behavior in half, washing only three times. These are realistic goals, and these goals can be expanded over time.

Some obsessive issues are more serious, though. The threat of terrorist attacks or catastrophic weather can cause people who have never had any sort of anxiety disorders to become stressed and fearful. To someone with an anxiety disorder, though, someone who becomes obsessed and stressed over something as nonthreatening as cans on the pantry shelf not being in order, the idea of a terrorist attack or a hurricane can be especially terrifying, even if there is no imminent threat. There are ways to cope with issues even this serious, though. First, it is important to understand the difference between facts and fears. One way to do this is to determine exactly how unlikely something like this is to happen.

One successful approach to coping with anxious feelings is to be proactive. For instance, someone who worries over the safety of family members can develop a disaster-readiness plan, which would include a list of food items and other supplies that would help the family be more safe and secure in the event of a hurricane or some other type of catastrophic weather. Developing a plan such as this is one way of taking positive action. Also, many families have a fire escape plan, which includes a meeting place outside the home where everyone should gather in the event of a fire, or a neighbor who would serve as a contact person if your family members became separated. Taking action and having a plan makes people feel more in control of their lives and more secure.

Another way to ease periods of anxiety is through visualization. Visualization is a way to temporarily send the mind to a "happy place." This happy place can be anywhere that the person considers relaxing and calm. The idea is to visualize

A good coping skill for a person with an anxiety disorder is to keep writing down an obsessive word or phrase for about a week. After this time the thought should not cause as much anxiety.

the place and imagine actually being there. This place can be a cabin in the mountains, a quiet beach, or even a favorite park. This technique takes time and effort, but with practice it is possible to change a state of anxiety to a calm, restful state. When a person becomes really successful with this skill, tense muscles loosen; shallow, rapid breathing is replaced by deep, relaxing breaths; the pulse slows; and the blood pressure comes down.

Some people with anxiety disorders help themselves by literally overdosing on worrisome thoughts. There are several ways to do this. One is to set aside daily worry time. This is a prearranged period of time when the person allows himself to dwell on depressing or stressful thoughts and consider worst-case scenarios of a specific issue or event. During this time, the person concentrates on becoming distressed. After a week or so of focusing on obsessive thoughts about this single issue, the person may run out of worries. Another way is to write down an obsessive word or thought and record a loop tape of it. After listening to this loop tape for thirty to forty-five minutes a day for a week or so, the obsessive thought should no longer cause anxiety.

Other strategies for coping on a daily basis include re-membering that, although these symptoms of anxiety issues such as panic and obsessive thoughts are frightening, they are neither dangerous nor harmful, and that these feelings of anxiety are just the mind and body's exaggerated reaction to something stressful. Sometimes, it is helpful to rate the fear level from zero to ten and watch it like an observer. Usually, the anxiety or fear will not stay at a high level for a very long period of time. Also, it is helpful to remember that the more willing a person is to face fears, the less threatening those fears become.

In addition to practicing self-help techniques, it is also im-portant to remember that anxiety disorders might remain part of a person's life to some degree. One person with a history of mild anxiety disorders describes how she has come to terms with these feelings:

I had gone through a few years of therapy as an adult, learning to cope with stressful issues in my adult life; things that had nothing to do with my childhood. What I learned was, anxiety issues had been pretty much a lifetime thing for me. As a kid in a working-class family in the 50s, separation anxiety and OCD—well—we'd never even heard of those things. Thanks to the therapy, I finally got it! I finally understood. I had thought I was just weird; maybe a little crazy. I thought I was the only one in the whole world like this. Now that's a pretty lonely feeling for a kid. Turns out I've been in pretty good company all these years. There are some pretty well-known people out there who are working through some of the same problems I've had. A relief? You just don't know!"[11]

Laughing off Anxiety

Approaching daily life and all of its challenges with humor can actually help people cope with anxiety. Humor distracts the mind from stressful, anxiety-causing issues and events. In fact, some experts believe that laughter produces endorphins, which ease pain and promote relaxation.

Young people as well as adults can look for humor in everyday situations. They can also generate laughter by watching funny movies and television programs, reading the comics in the daily newspaper, and even creating cartoons of their own, turning potentially stressful situations into something they can laugh at and put into perspective.

Laughter can help reduce stress, lower blood pressure, and boost the immune system. It is also good for the heart and makes a person feel good. Laughter is one contagious condition people do not mind catching.

Regaining Emotional Health as a Family

Any illness, mental or physical, does not just affect the individual, it affects the entire family. Because of this, other family members may need counseling just as much as the person with the disorder. For example, if a family member has OCD, parents and siblings genuinely want to help their loved one. However, the family needs to understand that participating in rituals, like repeatedly checking doors, windows, and appliances, or making sure that the person does not touch

Family therapy promotes support for people with anxiety disorders and aids the rest of the family with coping with the patient's illness.

certain objects and become upset does nothing to help that person cope with OCD. Helping the patient avoid a problem situation in the short term actually causes harm in the long term. Playing along enables the person to continue with the obsessive ritual or behavior. With the best of intentions, the family may believe that the condition will worsen if they do not participate in the rituals.

To help break this ritualistic cycle, the patient's therapist works with the patient to help him understand that he should not try to get family members to participate in the rituals and with the patient's family members to encourage them to refuse to participate if the patient tries to pull them back into the cycle. The patient's family needs to understand that their loved one needs to learn how to face difficult situations. Otherwise, the patient remains dependent on the family and does not learn how to overcome the inappropriate behavior.

The family needs to learn how to provide effective support, because, despite the desire to help, acting on the wrong information or responding in the wrong way can have a very negative outcome for the patient as well as the patient's family. Family members need to educate themselves. They need to learn the types of anxiety disorders, their symptoms, and appropriate types of treatment. Family members must not be afraid to talk openly about the condition with the patient, when that person is ready to discuss it, and to not pass judgment. They need to understand that emotional highs and lows are to be expected as their loved one progresses toward recovery and that feelings of frustration are normal. Family members can lend support by driving the person to therapy appointments, if the person has no transportation, and making sure the person knows that the disorder does not change the way family and friends feel about him or her, and, above all, family and friends need to be patient during what could be a lengthy treatment process.

Additionally, the family can celebrate the small successes, like daily goals, together. In this way, they are actively participating in a supportive way, acting as their loved one's cheering squad. They can help their loved one identify signs of backsliding into negative habits and remind him or her of steps to help manage these lapses. These support aids and other types of encouragement help keep the negative, stressful feelings from returning. However, family members must not take on the role of therapist. Their roll is supportive, to help their loved one maintain the improvements achieved during treatment.

As family members are showing support for their loved one, though, they may need to go into therapy themselves. Family therapy helps the family understand and cope with the patient's anxiety disorder. It promotes working together as a team, rather than assessing blame and finding fault, and can prove helpful in revealing issues in the parents' or siblings' behavior that may be contributing, even unintentionally, to the patient's anxiety.

Family therapy can be very useful in situations where the patient has been angrily lashing out at other family members, and the family has responded in kind, shouting back. Even if all involved understand that it is the anxiety and frustration caused by the disorder that is responsible for the shouting in the first place, nevertheless, these verbal assaults can result in hurt feelings all around. Family therapy can help repair this sort of emotional damage.

Another way family therapy can be helpful is when the anxiety disorder has caused a shift in family authority, where the child with the disorder has more or less taken control. For instance, if a child or teenage family member has been acting out and the adult family members have been constantly giving in to that person and letting him have his way, this harms relationships and causes resentment among other siblings. Sometimes, the parents feel that it is simply easier to ignore a son or daughter's inappropriate behavior or give in to it, rather than confront it. In situations like these, the young person with the disorder is the one in control of the family, not the parents. If nothing is done to correct it, these hard feelings can carry over into adulthood, because when the resentment continues in this way, it can either damage lifelong relationships or destroy them entirely. Family therapy can help the family reestablish normal, healthy dynamics, in which the parent, not the child, calls the shots and sets the boundaries.

Being a parent is a hard job. There are challenges and difficulties in raising children when those children have no psychological or physical problems. If one of the parents or one of the children has a physical or a mental disorder, this places a great deal of stress on the other parent and the other family members. There is no shame in seeking therapy or other kinds

Keeping an Anxiety Journal

Students are frequently required to keep journals. In fact, a journal might be part of a major grade. However, journals have many uses outside the classroom. Some people write about their vacations in journals, to help them remember especially good times. Journals can also be a tool to help people cope with anxiety. Some therapists ask their patients to keep journals as a part of their treatment, with the understanding that the patients have total control of the journal. The patients decide whether or not anyone else is allowed to read what is written in the journals. Since the patients have complete control of their journal, the therapists urge the patients to not hold back, to freely express feelings and to be totally honest.

A good way to begin a journal is by setting aside time in the evening and writing about the day's activities, describing feelings and thoughts that accompanied the day's events. Some entries may be longer than others, but it is important to write daily. After a few weeks, it is possible to look back through the entries and identify some of the actions, objects, or events that may be contributing to anxiety and personal actions that might have been helpful in overcoming anxious feelings.

of help when the family is coping with the physical or mental illness of a parent or a child.

Anxiety Disorder Support Groups

In addition to individual and family therapy, support groups can be a lifeline for patients and families who are recovering from anxiety disorders or who are learning to cope while in the process of healing. Support groups are not therapy and are not intended to take the place of therapy. However, these groups are helpful in addition to therapy. Even while undergoing treatment, people with anxiety disorders and their families can feel very isolated. They sometimes feel as though there is no one else who could possibly understand how they feel. In support groups, patients and their families can get information about local re-sources. They can meet people with some of the same symptoms and discuss which types of coping skills have and have not been successful for other patients and their family members.

There are several ways to locate support groups. The pro-fessional in charge of the family member's treatment can refer

Many anxiety patients participate in support groups, which should not be a substitute for therapy, but act as a place for people to share information.

both patients and families to groups. Another way to find a patient or family support group is by contacting the mental health departments of local hospitals. Many hospitals have support group meetings onsite. Churches, synagogues, and other faith-based organizations may also have such referral information. Mental health organizations are listed in telephone directories. These are good sources to check for support groups. Additionally, the library is a good source of information. Library books about mental health often have Web sites listed in the appendixes. Finally, school counselors often have a listing of support groups, which they will make available to parents upon request.

Some people, however do not live in an area where local support groups are available. This does not mean they do not have access to support organizations they need, though. A number of support groups are available online for people who have no such groups in their communities or for people who do not have access to transportation. Several issues should be considered in choosing an online support group. For safety and security reasons, online support groups should require a login and a valid e-mail address in order to join. For privacy, participants should be able to use screen names, and the site should be constantly moderated. If the patient has any concerns about a specific online group, it is best to ask his or her therapist or doctor. In fact, it is a good idea for the patient to consult the medical professional most familiar with his or her case before joining such a group. Therapists and doctors should be able to provide information about the online support groups best suited to their patients' needs and those sponsored by reputable organizations.

There are a number of online support groups sponsored by reputable organizations. For instance, Freedom From Fear (www.freedomfromfear.org) has links to blogs, help resources, and educational information. Another online source, www.healingwell.com, provides access to chat rooms twenty-four hours a day, seven days a week. Additionally, an online community called the Anxiety Community (www.anxietyhelp.org)

includes a forum, a chat room, articles, treatment information, and educational resources. Another online group, Find the Light (www.findthelight.net) is a support resource for people dealing with anxiety disorders, depression, and/or substance abuse problems. This Web site includes an online support forum, a recommended reading list, and other educational tools. These are just a few examples of online support groups. As previously suggested, though, it is best if a patient consults with his or her physician or therapist before becoming involved with any support group, online or local.

CHAPTER FIVE

Research and Looking Ahead

There is a saying: Today's science fiction is tomorrow's science. If this is true, there may, indeed, one day be a medication, or some other type of treatment that provides an instant cure for anxiety disorders as well as other mental disorders. Until then, though, scientists, doctors, and therapists will continue researching medications and other types of treatment to help people overcome anxiety disorders. From blood tests to gene therapy and virtual reality, many new developments in the treatment of anxiety disorders are showing positive results and providing encouragement for people affected by these conditions.

Research in Genetics and Gene Therapy

Gene therapy is a medical therapy in which altered genetic material is placed into living cells. Many scientists work from the premise that some forms of anxiety disorders are genetic in origin, so gene therapy is being evaluated as a way to treat anxiety disorders. In gene therapy, genetic engineering is used to transplant genes in an effort to cure a disease. Genetic engineering is the science of developing and applying technologies that alter genetic material. By altering genetic material, unfavorable cellular traits that make a person more susceptible to physical and psychiatric illnesses can be

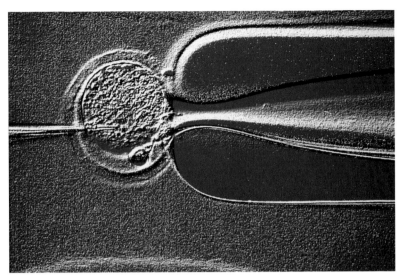

A scientist injects DNA into a cell in order to modify its genetic material. Researchers who believe that anxiety disorders are genetic in origin hope to use gene therapy as a way to treat the illness.

modified, decreasing the chances of the person developing a serious mental or physical condition.

The idea that certain people carry genes that make them more likely to have certain psychiatric and medical conditions goes back many years, but London researcher Jonathan Flint and his colleagues at the Wellcome Trust Center for Human Genetics, in Oxford, England, made significant progress in proving this idea, beginning in the early 1990s. They started tracking genetic effects in mice. They performed what is called an open field test, which is simply tracking a mouse's movements for five minutes in a brightly lit, unfamiliar environment, which for some mice is quite stressful. They discovered that, in stressful situations, mice behave much as humans do. The more anxious ones tended to cower, hiding and avoiding the environment as much as they could. Then, the scientists studied the genes of each generation of these mice, comparing the genes of those who appeared more anxious with the genes of those who behaved more calmly. They examined eighty-four genetic markers, finding three that appeared to account for the variations in behavior.

A genetic marker is a gene or DNA sequence that has an identified location on a chromosome and is associated with a certain trait. DNA is deoxyribonucleic acid, the material responsible for the genetic characteristics in all life forms. These genetic markers can be detected in blood tests to determine if a person is at risk of developing a certain disease or condition.

Another series of studies were done in the late 1990s. In this instance, though, the research subjects were human. Geneticist Xavier Estavill and psychiatrist Antonio Bulbena, both of Barcelona, Spain, studied the genome of ninety-three people from the same region who were affected by anxiety disorders. Among this group of people, the scientists found a particular region of chromosome that was duplicated and had high numbers of repetitive sequences called duplicons. This bit of genetic information, apparently a mutation, was named DUP25. They found DUP25 in 67, or 72 percent, of the test subjects. To gain further information, they tested another group of 70 people with anxiety disorders who were not all from the same region. This same DUP25 mutation was found in 68 of these individuals.

Dr. Estavill described the importance of these findings: "The identification of DUP25 opens a new era for the understanding of psychiatric disorders, which should lead to new definitions of the biological, genetic, and clinical basis of anxiety disorders."[12]

Although some of this research has been conducted in the past ten years, scientists have long known certain facts about genetic links, such as the more closely related a person is to someone with an anxiety disorder, the greater the chances are of that person already having or developing one or more anxiety disorders. Some studies have been done on identical twins in which one twin has an anxiety disorder. According to study results, the twin that does not suffer from an anxiety disorder has about a 50 percent chance of exhibiting anxiety disorder symptoms similar to the other twin. This has proven true even in situations where twins were separated as infants and raised in different households.

Research on identical twins have found that if one twin has an anxiety disorder, there is a 50 percent chance of the other twin exhibiting similar symptoms even if the twins were not raised together.

While these studies provide much useful information, there is still a great deal of work to be done in studying the variety of genetic markers that indicate the likelihood of a person having or developing an anxiety disorder. Possibly, in the future, parents will have access to this genetic information about their unborn children's chances for having an anxiety disorder, which could give them a valuable head start in understanding what sort of environment their children will need and what kinds of treatments will provide the best and earliest interventions.

Finding Other Clues in the Body

Some new blood tests and tests for chemicals in the brain can indicate the presence of or the tendency to develop certain anxiety disorders. In 2007, results of a study done through the

University of Iowa in which immature blood cells from sixteen people with panic disorder and from seventeen who did not have panic disorder provided some valuable information about diagnosing panic disorder. In the blood samples of those people with panic disorder, specific repetitive gene patterns were detected. Upon the completion of this investigation, the discovery of these patterns will be helpful in telling the difference between panic disorder and other health conditions.

According to Dr. Robert Philibert, a professor of psychiatry at the University of Iowa, "the ability to test for panic disorder is a quantum leap in psychiatry. Panic disorder will no longer be a purely descriptive diagnosis, but, as with cystic fibrosis, Down syndrome, and other conditions, a diagnosis based on genetic information. In addition, the finding could help us better understand the pathways that initiate, promote, and maintain panic disorder."[13]

The results of this study led the University of Iowa to begin working on a blood test for panic disorder. Since a number of the symptoms are quite similar for a panic attack and a heart

New blood tests have been developed to diagnose patients with anxiety disorders.

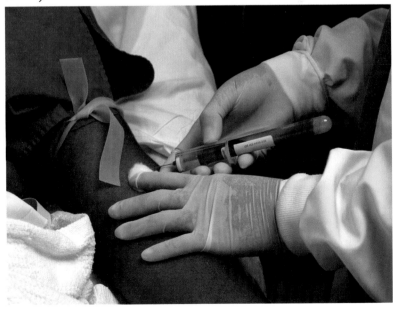

attack, this test can save a great deal of time in hospital emergency wards and quickly get patients on treatments that meet their needs.

Another blood test for diagnosing anxiety disorders has been developed at the Hebrew University, in Jerusalem. Spearheaded by Professor Hermona Soreq, dean of the faculty of science, the research for this study was based on test results from 461 volunteers from the United States. The participants were two-generation Caucasian and African American families. To determine if the volunteers had anxiety symptoms, they underwent a group of psychological tests. They also had very detailed blood tests. Professor Soreq and her team tried to determine if there was a connection between high levels of the enzymes and neurotransmitters, acetylcholinestrease (AChE), butyrylcholinestrease (BChE), and paraoxonase (PON) in the blood and anxiety. They discovered a correlation of greater than 90 percent. These tests further helped identify four main groups of people who have a higher than average tendency for developing anxiety disorders. As anticipated, two groups were women and people who had suffered previous traumas. The other two groups were African Americans and people with low body mass index (BMI).

Professor Soreq has high hopes for the future of this blood test. She says it should be accurate, inexpensive, and results of the tests should be ready within a matter of hours, rather than days.

In addition to blood tests, scientists are examining chemicals in the brain to see if the natural production of some of these chemicals can be modified to reduce anxiety and depression. A brain imaging study performed at the National Institutes of Health's National Institute of Mental Health (NIMH) has revealed the effect of the hormone, oxytocin, on the brain's fear hub, called the amygdala. It appears to be especially active in people with social phobia.

NIMH's director, Dr. Elias Zerhouni, describes the impact of this discovery: "Studies in animals, pioneered by now NIMH director, Dr. Thomas Insel, have shown that oxytocin plays a key role in complex emotional and social behaviors, such as attachment, social recognition, and aggression. Now, for the first time, we can literally see the same mechanisms at work in the human brain."[14]

To test the relationship between oxytocin and fear, fifteen volunteers, all healthy men, were asked to sniff oxytocin or a placebo before being examined by a magnetic resonance imaging (MRI) scan. This scan reveals which of the brain's parts are influenced by certain activities. During the scanning procedure, the men's brains responded to pictures showing threatening or fearful things. When the men who had received the placebo viewed the pictures, the amygdala responded strongly. There was much less response among the men who had received the oxytocin. This was especially noted when the men viewed photographs of threatening faces, which suggests the value of oxytocin in helping to manage social fears.

Robotic Psychotherapy?

Will there ever be a time when robots work as psychotherapists? In a way, this has already happened. New York City College of Technology's professor Adrianne Wortzel has created a virtual robot therapist, Eliza Redux. The robot therapist is programmed to move and to answer questions from anyone with an Internet connection. Upon logging in, the "patient" enters the virtual waiting room while waiting for a five-minute session. This virtual therapist is not actually performing psychotherapy, though. The Web site and the character of Eliza are actually a tribute to Professor Joseph Weisenbaum, who created the first computer program that mimics human conversation. So, although robotic psychotherapy is science fiction today, it may be reality one day in the future, considering the fact that robots are already performing some types of surgery.

Treating Anxiety Disorders with Virtual Reality

Help in the treatment of anxiety disorders is also coming from a source that seems more science fiction than science. Virtual reality is a computer-generated setting where humans can participate and interact to a certain degree within an artificial or virtual environment. This technology can involve many of the senses, including hearing, touch, sight, and in some instances, even smell. A virtual reality system has three parts. The first part is a fast, powerful computer called a reality simulator, which can run a virtual reality program fast enough so that there are no delays in interaction with the user. Within this simulator is the graphics board that produces the visual three-dimensional environment, the sound processors, and the controllers, for the input and output devices that connect the user

Although researchers started to use virtual reality to treat soldiers with post-traumatic stress disorder, many psychologists are now using virtual reality to treat many different types of anxiety disorders.

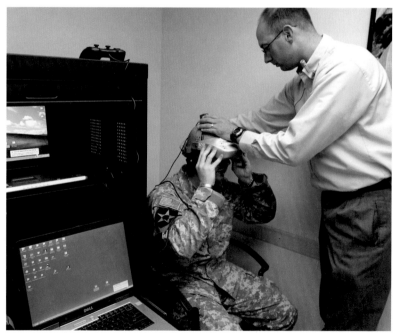

with the virtual environment. The second part consists of the input and output devices, called effectors. Effectors include head mounted displays (HMD), joysticks, and wired gloves. The final part of the virtual reality system is the user, the person interacting with the virtual environment.

Since every element of the virtual environment can be controlled, this technology can be a useful tool in helping people overcome some symptoms of their anxiety disorders. It has the potential of being especially helpful in exposure therapy, also called image flooding. In this type of therapy, patients are conducted through imaginary situations that bring on strong emotional responses, such as the fear and anxiety they experience when they are exposed to objects or events associated with their phobias, like driving cars or being in high places. During the session, they are not allowed to use the avoidance strategies they usually rely on in real situations. What makes virtual reality especially effective is that, although it places patients in lifelike situations, the therapist is in total control of the virtual environment and can adjust the intensity of the emotionally threatening element. Nothing will happen that is not programmed by the therapist.

Virtual reality as therapy is important in several ways. It can be less expensive than other types of therapy. There are several distinct benefits to the person receiving the treatment. The patient is spared the potential embarrassment of going through exposure therapy in public, the most anxiety-provoking aspects of situations and events such as war trauma, accidents, crowded places, and simulated takeoffs in aircraft can be replayed over and over to the point that these anxiety-causing issues become less threatening, and the therapist can instantly end the virtual experience if it should become too stressful for the patient. The patient experiences the anxiety of the event, but it takes place in the safety of a virtual environment.

Virtual reality is not in wide use for treating anxiety disorders at this time. It's potential usefulness is still under investigation. However, at some time in the future, virtual reality might become a standard form of treatment.

Clinical Trials

Many types of treatments and drugs for mental conditions as well as physical diseases are developed through a process called a clinical trial. A clinical trial is a scientific investigation of a drug, a device used in an invasive medical treatment, or a type of therapy, before it goes on the market or is used by the medical community. In the earliest stages, test subjects are usually animals, such as mice or rats. If these early investigations are successful, trials move on to human subjects. In some trials, subjects are paid for their time, but in others they are not. Trials vary in size from one researcher in one hospital working with a few test subjects to worldwide research facilities and thousands of subjects. Clinical trials are usually lengthy procedures, lasting months or even years. Human test subjects can be male or female, children, teens, adults, or

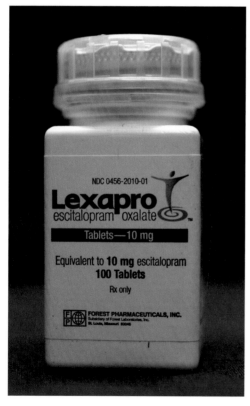

The antidepressant Lexapro is currently being studied as a treatment for general anxiety disorder in the elderly.

Flashbacks and the Brain

Researchers may have discovered what causes people with post-traumatic stress disorder (PTSD) to experience flashbacks. In recent years, psychiatrists studied a group of two dozen volunteers, each of whom had experienced some type of severe trauma. Of this group a little less than half developed PTSD and a little more than half did not. In order to learn why some people develop PTSD, the researchers studied the brain activity of each volunteer by using a functional magnetic resonance imaging (MRI) device.

One at a time, the volunteers were connected to the MRI so the researchers could monitor brain activity. While on the MRI, each volunteer was instructed to think about the traumatic event she had experienced. The researchers discovered that the people with PTSD were thinking with the right side of their brains, the part involved in nonverbal memory. On the other hand, the people who did not develop PTSD were thinking with the left side of their brains, the part associated with verbal memory. According to the scientists involved in the study, the activation of nonverbal memory may explain the flashbacks.

seniors, depending on the type of study. Finally, since volunteers usually need to be evaluated in person during the trial, they are usually required to live somewhere in the vicinity of the research facility involved in the clinical trial.

Some clinical trials performed in the past couple of years involving anxiety orders include studies of generalized anxiety disorder (GAD) and social anxiety disorder (SAD) and preventing anxiety disorders in young people and people in early middle age. Sponsored by the National Institute of Mental Health, the generalized anxiety and social anxiety disorders study recruited volunteers for their investigation in December 2006. To qualify, potential volunteers had to be between eighteen and fifty years old and in good physical health with an intelligent quotient (IQ) greater than eighty. They were interviewed by telephone and were required to complete a questionnaire. Those accepted had to make three visits to the National Institutes of Health Clinical Center. During the first visit, they answered questions about mood, nervousness, behavior, and thinking skills. Then, they underwent a complete physical examination, including an EKG, blood work, urinalysis, and if the volunteer was a female of childbearing years, a pregnancy test. On the second visit, the volunteers spent two and a half hours connected to electrodes to monitor electricity on the surface of the skin, performing a selection of tasks while seated and viewing a computer screen. The tasks evoked specific kinds of thoughts and feelings. On the third visit, volunteers performed the same tasks, only this time while lying in an MRI scanner. The purpose of this study was to evaluate the impact of GAD and SAD on processing information and learning.

Preventing Anxiety Disorders in Youth is another study sponsored by NIMH. In this study, researchers evaluated the usefulness of cognitive-behavior therapy in preventing anxiety disorders in at-risk children, primarily African Americans, who live in communities prone to violence. Both boys and girls, ages eight to twelve, were eligible for this study, which was carried out in the children's schools. Prior to this study, little research had been done in preventing anxiety disorders in children who live in areas noted for violence.

The children were assigned to either an anxiety prevention group or a nonintervention group for about three months. The prevention group received the therapy; the nonintervention group did not. At the end of the three months, parents and teachers were questioned about the anxiety symptoms of these children. They were questioned again during a follow-up visit after six months.

Another clinical trial is studying the effectiveness of a drug called escitalopram (Lexapro), an antidepressant and antianxiety drug, in treating GAD in elderly people. Participants in this study are sixty years old or older. Each participant has a weekly study visit for twenty-four weeks. For the first twelve weeks, the control group receives a placebo and a second group receives escitalopram. For the second twelve weeks, all participants receive escitalopram. During these visits, participants will complete questionnaires on functionality and anxiety symptoms. Blood samples will be taken, and the volunteers will be evaluated on certain tasks. This clinical study is important because GAD is most prevalent among the elderly, and anything that relieves the condition improves their quality of life and overall health. Although these studies are currently in the data-gathering stages and the volunteer portion of the trials may have been completed, scientists are very careful in their evaluations and it could be months or even years before the conclusions are revealed.

Getting the Word Out

Possibly two of the most important tools in battling anxiety disorders or any psychiatric condition are knowledge and communication. Trying to ignore their very real presence in society or avoiding talking about them do not make them go away. Educational programs, communication, and support networks play a vital role in understanding complex conditions of the mind. One of the largest programs currently underway to promote education and support for anxiety disorders and other forms of mental illness is through the National Alliance on Mental Illness (NAMI). NAMI C.A.R.E (Consumers Advocating Recovery through Empowerment) began in suburban Chicago, Illinois, and has already spread to a number of major cities. NAMI plans to expand the program to all fifty states and Puerto Rico. By 2009 they hope to have a support group in every major city in the United States, with training materials in both Spanish and English. AstraZeneca, a large international pharmaceutical and health-care business, is partnering in this effort.

Tony Zook, president and CEO of AstraZeneca says, "Because patient health is at the foundation of everything we do, we are pleased to be part of a program that will have a dramatic impact on the health of people with mental illness.

Our responsibility goes well beyond just making medicines. We are also committed to help making available the supportive services that patients need, also."[15]

Programs such as this one go a long way in providing support for people with anxiety disorders and other mental health issues and educating the general public about these conditions. Additionally, researchers in medicine, science, and technology are constantly upgrading medications, revising some types of therapies, and creating entirely new forms of therapy. While mental health disorders will probably never be completely eradicated, these advancements will greatly improve the quality of life for people affected by anxiety disorders and other mental health conditions.

Notes

Introduction: When Anxiety Becomes a Disorder

1. Quoted in HealthyPlace.com, "Famous People Who Have Experienced an Anxiety Disorder," HealthyPlace.com. www.healthyplace.net/communities/anxiety/paems/people/index.htm.
2. Quoted in HealthyPlace.com, "Famous People Who Have Experienced an Anxiety Disorder."

Chapter 1: What Are Anxiety Disorders?

3. Quoted in BrainPhysics Mental Health Resource, "Generalized Anxiety: An Overview," BrainPhysics Mental Health Resource Web site. www.brainphysics.com/generalized-anxiety.php.
4. Quoted in Fred Penzel, *Obsessive-Compulsive Disorder: A Complete Guide to Getting Well and Staying Well.* New York: Oxford University Press, 2000, p. 157.
5. Quoted in BrainPhysics Mental Health Resource, "Generalized Anxiety: An Overview."
6. Quoted in BrainPhysics Mental Health Resource, "Generalized Anxiety: An Overview."

Chapter 2: Patient Age and Family Relationships

7. Quoted in SeniorJournal.com, "'The Aviator' Draws Attention to Anxiety Disorders in Older Adults," SeniorJournal.com. www.seniorjournal.com/NEWS/Health/4-12-30Aviator.htm.
8. Quoted in Stephanie Sampson, "New Thinking on Anxiety and Aging: Anxiety Disorders Common in the Elderly," Anxiety Disorders Association of America. www.adaa.org/aboutADAA/newsletter/AnxietyandAging.htm.

Chapter 3: Diagnosis and Treatment

9. Quoted in Stephanie Sampson, "Anxiety in the Age of Innocence: Children and Anxiety Disorders," Anxiety Disorders Association of America. www.adaa.org/gettinghelp/newsletter/childrenAnxiety.asp.
10. Quoted in HealthyPlace.com, "Monoamine Oxidase Inhibitors," HealthyPlace.com. www.healthyplace.com/communities/depression/treatment/antidepressants/MAOI.asp.

Chapter 4: Coping with Anxiety and Anxiety Disorders

11. Author interview, October 2007. Name withheld by request.

Chapter 5: Research and Looking Ahead

12. Quoted in Xavier Bosch, "Anxiety Disorders Linked to Gene Abnormality," *British Medical Journal*, August 13, 2001. www.pubmedcentral.nih.gov/articlerender.fcgi?artid=1172910.
13. Quoted in Robert Preidt, "Blood Test Could Spot Panic Disorder." University of Iowa News Release, March 6, 2007.
14. Quoted in 4Therapy.com, "Brain Chemical Boosts Trust and Short-Circuits Fear," 4Therapy.com. www.4therapy.com/consumer/conditions/article/7970/73/Brain+Chemicals+Boosts+Trust+and +Short-Circuits+Fear.
15. Quoted in National Alliance on Mental Illness Web site "NAMI to Increase Support Groups Nationwide Through AstraZeneca Partnership". www.nami.org/Template.cfm?Section=press_room&template=/ContentManagement/ContentDisplay.cfm&ContentID=42705.

Glossary

agoraphobia: Abnormal fear of being in a helpless or embarrassing situation in a public place.

amygdala: An almond-shaped mass in the front of the temporal lobe of the brain that controls fear.

anxiety disorder: A general term for a group of mental disorders in which severe anxiety is a major symptom.

body dysmorphic disorder (BDD): The name of an anxiety-related condition in which a person has a distorted body image and is extremely critical of his or her self-image.

chromosome: A chromosome is a long piece of DNA in a cell's nucleus which carries genetic material.

clinical trial: A detailed investigation of a drug, a treatment, or a surgical device.

CT scan: Also called computed axial tomography, this is a device that uses X-rays to create detailed images of structures inside the body.

desensitization: A type of exposure therapy in which a patient is repeatedly exposed to the thought or image of a feared threat. This technique is used in the treatment of some anxiety disorders.

diabetes: A disease in which the blood's glucose, or sugar, levels are too high.

DNA: Deoxyribonucleic acid, a nucleic acid that carries genetic instructions for all living things.

duplicons: Duplicated DNA.

electrocardiogram (ECG): A graphic recording of the electrical impulses of the heart.

electroencephalogram (EEG): A graphic record of electrical activity in the brain.

enzymes: Proteins that originate in living cells.

flashback: An abnormally vivid recollection of a traumatic event.

generalized anxiety disorder (GAD): An anxiety disorder characterized by an overall anxious mood with chronic anxiety symptoms, such as sweating and lightheadedness.

genetic engineering: The use of scientific methods and technology to manipulate or alter genetic material.

genetic marker: A chromosomal indicator that enables tracking of specific genetic traits.

hallucinations: When the mind creates a realistic experience that is not actually occurring.

head mounted display (HMD): A device worn on the head that has an optic display positioned in front of each eye. Part of a virtual reality system.

hormone: A chemical message carrier that carries a signal through the blood from one cellular structure to another.

hyperglycemia: A high amount of glucose in the blood's plasma.

hypothesis: A prediction based on scientific information.

insomnia: Trouble falling asleep or staying asleep.

magnetic resonance imaging (MRI): A noninvasive medical test that allows doctors to see organs, soft tissues, and bones.

metabolism: Physical and chemical biological processes that allow the body to grow and mature, such as digestion.

monoamine oxidase inhibitors (MAOIs): A group of antidepressant drugs with potentially serious side effects.

neurotransmitters: Chemicals that relay signals to the brain.

norepinepherine: A neurotransmitter associated with alertness. It is produced from another neurotransmitter, dopamine.

obsessive-compulsive disorder (OCD): An anxiety disorder characterized by repetitive thoughts and actions.

panic attack: Sudden periods of extreme anxiety.

panic disorder: An anxiety disorder characterized by repeated periods of extreme anxiety and fear, with accompanying symptoms such as rapid pulse, shaking, and heavy perspiring.

phobia: The most common mental disorder, characterized by irrational fear of an activity, object, or situation.

post-traumatic stress disorder (PTSD): A psychological disorder caused by traumatic events.

psychotherapy: Treating psychological disorders with group therapy, behavioral therapy, or psychoanalysis.

selective mutism: A childhood anxiety disorder. The inability to speak in social settings.

selective serotonin reuptake inhibitors (SSRIs): A class of drugs used in the treatment of depression and OCD.

separation anxiety: Fear and anxiety that results from being separated from familiar people and settings.

serotonin: A neurotransmitter involved with sleep, depression, and memory.

tricylic antidepressants (TCAs): A group of antidepressants used in the treatment of depression and some anxiety disorders.

urinalysis: A test for examining the urine for general health and detecting the presence of drugs.

virtual environment: A computer-generated, three-dimensional environment.

virtual reality: A simulated environment created by a complex, three-part computer system.

Organizations to Contact

Anxiety Disorders Association of America
11900 Parklawn Dr., Suite 100
Rockville, MD 20852
(301) 231-0350
www.adaa.org

Founded in 1980, Anxiety Disorders Association of America is a nonprofit organization dedicated to educating both professionals and the public about anxiety disorders, treatment, and helping people find treatment programs in their home communities. It conducts an annual national conference as well as provides reference information on research.

Freedom From Fear
308 Seaview Ave.
Staten Island, NY 10305
(718) 680-1883
www.freedomfromfear.org

Established in 1984, Freedom From Fear began as a small support group. From its modest beginnings, Freedom From Fear has grown to include national outreach programs. It provides training for health-care professionals, produces educational television programs, establishes grants for research, and lobbies for government support.

National Institute of Mental Health (NIMH)
The Anxiety Disorders Education Program
5600 Fishers Lane
Room 7C-02 MSC 8030
Bethesda, MD 20892
(301) 443-4513
(888) 8-ANXIETY

The parent organization of NIMH, the National Institutes of Health, can be traced back to the late 1800s. NIMH supports mental health in a number of ways. Hundreds of scientists and researchers conduct clinical trials supported by NIMH. The organization supports outreach programs and publishes educational materials in both English and Spanish. It also provide updates on the latest scientific developments in mental health.

For Further Reading

Books

Nancy M. Campbell, *Panic Disorder*. Mankato, MN: Capstone Press, 2002. This book includes an explanation and definition of anxiety, fear, and panic. It also supplies information about types of treatment, the recovery process, and prevention measures.

Sucheta Connolly, David Simpson, and Cynthia Petty, *Anxiety Disorders*. New York: Chelsea House, 2006. Issues covered in this book include how anxiety disorders develop, the different types of anxiety disorders, evaluation, and treatment.

Charles H. Elliott and Laura L. Smith, *Anxiety and Depression Workbook for Dummies*. Hoboken, NJ: Wiley, 2006. This book deals with discovering the origins of a person's anxieties and approaches to self-help.

Edna B. Foa and Reid Wilson, *Stop Obsessing: How to Overcome Your Obsessions and Compulsions*. New York: Bantam, 2001. This books identifies compulsions and behaviors of OCD. It also provides suggestions of how to let go of worries and how to master obsessions. Some medications are described, as well.

M. Nikki Goldman, *Emotional Disorders*. New York: Marshall Cavendish, 1994. This volume provides a wealth of information on the causes of emotional disorders, including anxiety disorders, depression, and schizophrenia. It also describes both healthy and unhealthy ways of dealing with stress, and includes information on both professional and self-help.

Bruce M. Hyman and Cherry Pedrich, *Obsessive-Compulsive Disorder*. Brookfield, CT: Twenty-First Century Books, 2003. This book provides a detailed description of what OCD is, its symptoms, and different types of treatment currently available.

Sheila Wyborny, *Virtual Reality*. Detroit, MI: Blackbirch, 2003. This book offers the history of virtual reality as well as recent technological developments. It also discusses some directions virtual reality may take in the future.

Web Sites

Anxiety and Panic Pit Stop (http://members.tripod.com/ xanman22/index.html). This Web site describes the different types of anxiety disorders in easy-to-understand language. It has online resources categorized by the type of disorder and links to information about medications.

For Kids and Teens (www.ncpamd.com/kids_pages.htm). This site includes reviews of children's books about mental health, activities, and articles written especially for young people about personal, sibling, and parental mental health problems.

NIEHS Kids' Pages (http://kids.niehs.nih.gov/music.htm). Music has been proven to ease pain and relieve anxiety. This site has music and lyrics, sing-along style, to many popular songs for children and teens, including patriotic, religious, and popular tunes.

Index

Picture Credits

About the Author

Sheila Wyborny is a retired middle school teacher. She and her husband, a consulting engineer, live in a private airport community in Cypress Texas.